Montessori
PLAY & LEARN

Montessori
PLAY & LEARN

A Parents' Guide to Purposeful Play from Two to Six

LESLEY BRITTON
With an Introduction by Joy Starrey Turner

Crown Publishers, Inc.
New York

Editorial Note:
To avoid stereotyping, general references to children are alternated between he and she section by section in this book.

Designer: Peter Butler
Photographer: Ron Sutherland
Illustrator: Gillian Hurry

Published by Crown Publishers, Inc.,
201 East 50 Street, New York, New York 10022.
Member of the Crown Publishing Group.

CROWN is a trademark of Crown Publishers, Inc.

Library of Congress Cataloging-in-Publication Data

Britton, Lesley.
    Montessori play and learn : a parent's guide to purposeful play from two to six / Lesley Britton.
        p.   cm.
    1. Montessori method of education – Handbooks, manuals, etc.   2. Play – Handbooks, manuals, etc.
    3. Teaching – Aids and devices – Handbooks, manuals, etc.   4. Education, Preschool – United States – Parent participation – Handbooks, manuals, etc.   I. Title.
    LB775.M8868   1992
    649'.68–dc20   92-5446
                                                      CIP

ISBN 0-517-59182-0

10 9 8 7 6 5 4 3 2
First Edition

Typeset in England by Servis Filmsetting Ltd.
Printed and bound in Portugal by
Printer Portuguesa, Lda.

ACKNOWLEDGMENTS

This book could not have been written without the support and cooperation of many people. I especially wish to acknowledge my thanks to my editor, Isabel Moore, whose unfailing support and encouragement have been vital in seeing the book through. I would also like to acknowledge the contribution made by Nicky Adamson to the section on Planning Your Home Around Your Child. For their assistance in the design and illustration of the book, I am grateful to Peter Butler for his excellent design, to Ron Sutherland for his superb photographs, to Gillian Hurry for her illustrations and to Becky and Chris Ellis for the kind loan of their home for photography.

I am particularly grateful to Martina Furness, principal of the nursery school at the London Montessori Centre, and to the children of the school, without whose contribution the book could not have been completed. My special thanks, too, to Nienhuis Montessori International for allowing me to include and illustrate games from their Nienhuis Collection throughout the book.

Finally, I would like to thank my family: my husband, David Joffick, for his patience, and my three daughters, Juliette and Bettina Hohnen and Sophia Britton, for the joy they have given me over the years and for giving me the inspiration to study and practice the Montessori Method in the first place.

The photograph used on page 130 is used courtesy of the Science Photo Library.

NOTE: Games used in this book from the Nienhuis Collection can be obtained commercially from Nienhuis Montessori USA Inc. 320 Pioneer Way, Mountain View, California 94041.

CONTENTS

INTRODUCTION

Have today's parents lost the power to guide and influence their children? Faced with the mighty attractions of television, the competing pressures of school and peers, and the limited family time available to working parents, it is no wonder that many think so.

Yet the more we learn about humans, the more we become aware that no force in children's lives has more importance than parents. Parenting forms children's core belief about themselves; at the very beginning of their being, the way children see themselves mirrored in the eyes of their earliest caretakers and how their behavior is reflected back forms their image of who they are. Because children are any culture's greatest natural resource, the future of the world depends on our children's conceptions of themselves; all their choices come out of this self-view. And nothing could be more important than that.

The human family evolved as a social process to assure survival. Although the historical anxieties about physical survival may have been replaced by a new psychological/emotional level (parents now worry about things like drug use, delinquency, sexual aberration, academic and social failures), and although styles may have changed (moving away from tyranny and toward democracy), the parents' job is still the same.

Parents are still the child's first and most important teachers. Given this truth, it seems strange and also rather tragic that so many parents today consider teaching a prerogative exclusive to the school – no matter how clear it may become that schools often fail to meet our children's needs. In fact, schools may be one of the forces in our culture that stand in the way of a child's natural ability to learn. In a world that needs individual intelligence, energy, creativity, and cooperation more than ever, schools seem to perpetuate such barriers as competition, testing, grades, stress, shame, boredom, dull textbooks, bland teachers, student labeling, and educational tracking. No one denies that schools and parents must work in partnership to foster the child; but how can we give suport to institutions that so often disregard the facts of human development?

For parents who want to assist their children in realizing their full potential in life, I believe there are two things to do. One is to reclaim your franchise as your child's first and most natural teacher. The other is to support the public school reform movement currently incubating here.

According to one of my favourite public school principals (Sommer, 1992), the drive for educational reform has grown out of "effective schools" research of the past few decades and calls for the following:

- multi-age classrooms
- early childhood education
- a rich and extensive curriculum
- cross-discipline learning
- whole language
- writing before reading
- "whole-piece" exposure to classical literature
- testing by portfolio
- developing self-discipline
- teaching values
- using hands-on materials
- fostering scientific and mathematical aptitudes
- nurturing appreciation for history, timelines, and cultural differences past and present
- care of our global environment

— and all in a school setting with a "family atmosphere."

If your child happens to attend a *Montessori* school, you won't be surprised to hear that

Montessori lies ahead in the direction others now want to go, for these things are all being done, and done successfully, in the almost 5,000 Montessori schools in this country, as well as untold others in more than 80 countries around the world. For almost a century, Montessori education has been addressing the academic, social, physical, and emotional needs of children. What may surprise you is the idea that Montessori's success in nurturing development is probably due in large part to the fact that it is modeled on natural, family-like patterns of teaching-learning: the multi-age grouping of a Montessori class resembles family structure much more closely than the chronological age segregation of the traditional, graded school; the emphasis on a "prepared environment" resembles the modifications to the household made by most families when a new child enters.

But perhaps the most significant aspect is the adult-child interaction style of the Montessori system, which seems clearly derived from a family model. Described as the "natural learning cycle," the young child's attraction to learning a new skill seems to develop in five steps. First, the child *observes demonstrations*; that is, on more than one occasion, s/he watches as a trusted model performs a task the child is interested in mastering (for example, making peanut butter sandwiches). Second comes the *participation* stage: the child begins to interact (perhaps clumsily, at first) in the model's performance of the task, so that it becomes a collaborative effort suitable to the child's level of competence (helping by laying out slices of bread). The third step is practice; as in role-play, this is self-regulated repetition in which the child assumes responsibility for his or her actions, learns from trial and error, and moves toward refinement (is discovered in the kitchen surrounded by many trial sandwiches in various stages of preparation).

Then comes the *eureka moment*: the child achieves a sense of accomplishment, an "I know how to do this" feeling (proudly announcing s/he can make her/his own sandwich for lunch). This leads directly to the fifth step, *performance*: at this stage the child revels in his or her mastery by demonstrating the newly acquired skill, delights in showing off the new competence for all comers, and begins to use the task in a context of social purpose (offering to make sandwiches for the whole family and any guests who happen to be within range). The natural learning cycle is observable in almost any family with young children.

It is out of this "brand-new" but time-tested approach that *Montessori Play & Learn* has evolved. Although the author of this book is British, the specifics as well as the principles are equally applicable to American children – a fact that simply bears testimony to the accuracy of Dr. Montessori's insights about the universal characteristics of childhood. In straightforward but easygoing language, the book models all the important strategies that work so well in Montessori classrooms: observing and respecting your child's response to environments and people, arranging the home environment to facilitate your child's independence, using your home and neighborhood as sources of enjoyable learning activities, and teaching/reinforcing global values through cooperative projects with your child.

Children have strong inner motivation to learn, if the material is presented in a natural and unforced way. One of the most consistent research findings is the dramatic improvement in student motivation and achievement that seems to result from close parental involvement in their children's learning process. So perhaps the greatest promise of this book is that parents can become *aware* of the natural learning cycle as they interact with and observe their own children – and thus regain a sense of the power and influence they may *think* they have lost.

JOY STARREY TURNER, PRESIDENT, MONTESSORI ACCREDITATION COUNCIL FOR TEACHER EDUCATION

WHO WAS MARIA MONTESSORI?

Many people will have heard the name "Montessori" and probably associate it with kindergarten education. Indeed you may well have picked this book up in the first place because your child goes to a kindergarten purporting to use the Montessori Method. However, relatively few people really know what it means or much about its founder, Maria Montessori. If you wish to apply her method to the upbringing of your own children, it is worth knowing a little about her life and the influences that helped her develop her ideas about child rearing and early learning.

Born in 1870, in a place called Chiaravalle, in Italy, Maria Montessori was the only child of a middle-class family. Her father, an accountant, moved to Rome when she was twelve, which meant she could receive a good education which would prepare her for a teaching career, the only real profession open to educated young women at that time. As her studies developed, she showed an interest in the sciences, and out of this came a determination to become a doctor. It is ironic that as an adolescent she adamantly refused to follow her parents' wishes to become a teacher. She applied to the University of Rome and after battling against the prejudices of the late 19th century toward women and the opposition of her father, she gained entrance to the medical school in 1890. She eventually graduated to become the first woman Doctor of Medicine in Italy.

Upon graduating her first appointment was as an assistant in the San Giovanni Hospital, working with women and children. In 1897 she became a voluntary assistant at the psychiatric clinic of the University of Rome.

During this time she encountered the so-called "idiot children." These were feeble-minded children who, because they were unable to function in school or in their families, were put into asylums among the criminally insane. While she had been studying at the University, there had been much undergraduate discussion about socialism, and it is not surprising, therefore, that Montessori had a passionate interest in social reform. She was also a doctor interested in pediatrics, and so she was particularly sensitive to the plight of these children who were locked away with nothing to do and with no sensory stimulation of any kind. When they were taken food, they would throw themselves on the floor looking for crumbs. It occurred to her that this behavior was a distinct effort on their behalf to try to learn about the world around them through their *hands*. This idea, that the path to intellectual development is through the hands, is a major theme in her Method.

Montessori became convinced that these children were not useless – just that their minds had never been stimulated. She began to work with them at the clinic, and gradually discovered glimmers of hope as they responded to her efforts.

While searching for information about the treatment of mentally deficient children, she came across the work of two French doctors, Jean Itard and Edouard Seguin. Itard made a particular study of deaf mutes, but he is probably better known for his attempts, over several years, to educate and socialize a retarded boy found abandoned in the forests of Aveyron, in France.

A portrait of Maria Montessori by Sir Frank Salisbury. Her long life was dedicated to improving the education of children, starting from the early observation that every child spontaneously wants to learn. By the time she died, in 1952, her Method was being taught successfully throughout the world.

He wrote an account of his efforts in a book called *The Wild Boy of Aveyron*. His particular approach was to stimulate the boy's mind systematically through the senses.

Edouard Seguin was a student of Itard, and he later founded his own school for deficients in Paris. His particular approach was to devise a sequence of muscular exercises to bring about a change in behavior and so educate the child through a method he described as physiological.

The study of the work of these two French doctors gave Maria Montessori a new direction in her life. She took the principal ideas of "education of the senses" and the "education of movement," and adapted and developed them into a system that became her own.

Her next step was to turn her mind to the study of education. Methodically she read all the major works she could find on education theory that had been written in the previous two hundred years. Gradually some of the ideas and insights of educational thinkers and reformers such as Rousseau, Pestalozzi and Froebel became synthesized in her mind with the ideas she had taken from Itard and Seguin, and the beginning of the so called "Montessori Method" was taking shape. What she, in fact, accomplished was to draw together the knowledge and methods from the disciplines of education and medicine.

By 1899 she was involved in the establishment of the Orthophrenic School in Rome, where she spent two years with colleagues, training teachers in the special method of observation and education of the mentally retarded. During this time she worked with the children, observing and experimenting, using different materials and methods, and employing the ideas she had gleaned from her studies. Some of the children she taught who had been labeled "uneducable" learned to read and write; some even sat the State primary examinations and passed with higher grades than so-called "normal" children. These events, together with the many public lectures she gave in Italy and other European countries,

brought her fame. What is more she was now known as an "educator" as well as a "doctor."

In 1901 Maria Montessori gave up her work at the Orthophrenic School in order to further her studies in anthropology, psychology and educational philosophy at the University of Rome. However, according to one of her biographers, Rita Kramer, there was another reason. The importance of mentioning it here is that this event may have had a profound effect on her life and consequently been another major turning point. It is claimed that she gave birth to an illegitimate child, Mario Montessori, around this period and that the father was none other than her colleague at the Clinic, Dr. Montesano. Mario was brought up by foster parents, but later was adopted by his mother. Kramer asserts that Maria Montessori "deprived of the experience of caring for her own child turned her attention increasingly to ways of meeting the needs of other children."

While studying and preparing herself for a career in education, Montessori visited many schools, observing both the methods used and the reactions of children. She was appalled at what she saw and this helped to crystallize her belief in the ideas of the educational thinkers who were forerunners of the "progressive movement" in education. The most significant influence on her was probably Friedrich Froebel, although she was also influenced by an anthropologist, Guiseppe Sergi, whom she credited with being responsible for turning her attention to the importance of the school environment and the role it could play in changing the child's behavior.

In 1904 she was appointed Professor of Pedagogic Anthropology at the University, and at the same time continued with her many other activities.

In 1906, Montessori was asked to organize the infant schools being built in a slum clearance and rehousing project. The first school, a large tenement house in San Lorenso, was for children aged three to six. She called it "*Casa dei Bambini*," the Children's House in Italian.

In the following two years, other children's houses were founded. In these schools Montessori was now able to apply her methods to normal children. She believed that if her methods achieved such startling results with retarded children, then these same methods would improve the performance of normal children.

The children in her first two children's houses were what we would now call deprived. They were often neglected, and lacked care and stimulation from their parents. In many cases, the parents themselves were illiterate. Under Montessori's care, these children began to learn successfully. In another school, children from relatively privileged backgrounds also proved that Montessori's methods were much superior to the conventional teaching of her day. It was soon evident, in fact, that all children were capable of achieving and becoming independent learners when taught by her methods. Montessori's hopes were realized.

International fame and recognition now came quickly. The world's press disseminated many stories of how successful her methods were, and within a few years she was internationally known. In 1909 her book, *The Method of Scientific Pedagogy as Applied to Infant Education and the Children's House*, which described in detail her method for schools, was published. It was later retitled *The Discovery of the Child* and translated into over twenty languages. It remains in print to this day.

Visitors came from many parts of the world to see for themselves the successful and stimulating teaching and learning taking place in the children's houses. They were inspired by what they saw and conveyed the word when they returned home. In this way, the Montessori movement spread all over the world, with schools opening in places as widely separated as North America, Japan, Germany and India, to name only some.

Montessori now spent all her time on her new work, training teachers, writing and giving lectures. She traveled extensively, visiting the newly founded schools and Montessori societies. In the U.S., particularly, her ideas were widely acclaimed. She was received in the White House and Margaret Wilson the daughter of President Woodrow Wilson, became a trustee of the Montessori Educational Association sponsored by Alexander Graham Bell.

In the early 1920s, Montessori was appointed Government Inspector of Schools for Italy. She did not hold the post for long because of her disagreement with the Fascist government. She spent some time in Spain, where she founded a special Teacher Training Institute in Barcelona. With the growing political tensions in that part of Europe in the '30s, she left Spain to live in Holland. By 1939 she was in India, where she remained throughout the war years, developing the movement in that subcontinent.

When her internment ended in 1946, she visited England and revived interest in the movement there. For the next few years, despite advancing years, she continued to travel extensively, teaching and lecturing, and she was honored by many countries with royal, civic and academic awards. She died in Holland in 1952.

Following her death, the movement continued to grow steadily. By the early 1960s the growth had accelerated and there was a worldwide revival of interest in her ideas that has continued to the present day. In the United States, by the early 1990s, there were over four thousand Montessori schools. Likewise, in Britain, the growth of interest in Montessori has been rapid and continuous. This expansion will undoubtedly continue in the future because Montessori training programs have started up all over the world. In October 1991 all the major groups met in New Orleans, and an umbrella organization was formed called "The Montessori Accreditation Council for Teacher Education." This is a major step forward, which now guarantees a united cooperative effort to promote the Montessori Method internationally.

THE ESSENCE OF THE MONTESSORI METHOD

In order to incorporate Montessori ideas into your own family environment, you need to have some knowledge of her basic philosophy of child development. As you will see later in this book, it is not so very different from those of modern experts; and once the terms are explained, it is easy to apply them to your own everyday life.

Maria Montessori drew her ideas about how to handle and educate children from her observations of them at different stages in their development, and from her exposure to children of different cultures. She identified what she saw that was common in all children as "the universal characteristics of childhood," regardless of where children were born or how they were brought up. She then set out to act as an interpreter for children everywhere, advising adults to adopt a new approach to them and treat the period of childhood as an entity in itself, not merely a preparation for adulthood.

These can be summed up as follows:

- All children have "absorbent" minds

- All children pass through "sensitive" periods

- All children want to learn

- All children learn through play/work

- All children pass through several stages of development

- All children want to be independent

Since they together form the core of belief upon which the Montessori Method is based, it is worth looking at each one in more detail.

THE ABSORBENT MIND

A child is fundamentally different from an adult in the way he learns. He has what Montessori called an *absorbent mind*, one that unconsciously soaks up information from the environment, learning about it at a rapid rate. This capacity to learn in this way is unique to the young child and lasts for the first six years of his life, more or less. During this time, the impressions made on the child's mind actually shape and form it, and therefore have an impact on his future development. It follows, therefore, that each and every early experience is of vital importance; this is especially so in the first phase of the *absorbent mind* – birth to three – when conscious learning has not yet emerged.

Take, for example, the way a child learns language. His parents do not teach him – language is acquired without effort, and literally sinks in. Less obviously, he acquires the social and cultural norms of his group in this way, too. Babies born in China, America, Africa or Europe will all be more or less the same at birth, except perhaps for some facial characteristics or skin color, but in the first few years, and certainly by the age of six, they will all have learned to speak their mother tongue, and they will all show different types of behavior conforming to their own particular social and cultural group.

The Conscious Mind

In the second phase – three to six – the child's mind is still *absorbent*, but now *consciousness* begins to appear. This comes partly with knowledge and partly with language. Also at this time his *will* begins to appear. With the ability to control his actions – and, of course, the ability to say "no" – he now appears to know what he wants and he will have no hesitation in trying to get his own way. As this is also the phase when new skills are rapidly and easily acquired, you will be asked endless questions of the "why" and "how" variety; his mind is still *absorbent*, but now shows a conscious thirst for knowledge.

Do not assume from what I have already said that a child of this age has a mind like a blank sheet of paper, or an empty vessel that will be gradually filled up, absorbing indiscriminately from the outside world. The process of learning during this period is *active*, rather than *passive*. Your child has inborn drives and energies that have a say in what happens – rather like a blueprint. It follows that you should try to give him as much freedom as possible at this time to follow what interests him most. Only with this freedom can he develop to his full potential.

This is all very well in the controlled environment of the kindergarten school, but many parents find this idea very difficult to come to terms with in the home. Birth to six is also the period when children are most vulnerable and when they are in the greatest need of protection. It is much easier for you to say "no," "don't touch" or "don't do that" and so on until you feel that he is old enough to know what is safe, and what is right and what is wrong. Maria Montessori discovered, however, that with careful guidance a child can be taught by experience about safety at quite an early age.

You will see later how your home can be arranged to give your child more freedom than you may have thought possible. There are many games and activities that can help you teach your toddler or young child to treat with respect such things as hot pans and kettles, electric appliances, and so on. When you apply the ideas of Montessori, you will help him to develop the self-discipline he needs to avoid problems.

THE SENSITIVE PERIODS
From her observations of children, Montessori noticed that they seem to pass through phases when they keep repeating an activity time and

time again – for no apparent reason. They become totally absorbed by what they are doing, and, for the time being, this is the only thing in which they are interested.

This is easy to observe. On a shopping trip to the supermarket, for instance, you may notice that your two year old wants to touch everything in sight. He will go to the shelves, pick something up, look at it, feel it, turn it around, try to find out what it's for and what can be done with it. He probably does this over and over again, and you may find it difficult to prize him away when you are hurrying to get home – the resulting confrontation is fairly familiar to any parent. In this situation it can be a help to know that your child is not being deliberately "naughty" but is, according to Montessori, showing his predisposition to develop new knowledge and skills through his senses. He needs to explore everything – this is how he learns. In Montessori terms this is a "sensitive period."

Once he has acquired adequate knowledge of the world, the phase passes and there is no longer an uncontrollable desire to touch everything. But if too many restrictions are placed on the child and his natural instincts are stunted while he is in this phase, he may throw tantrums to show you that he has an unsatisfied need to learn.

Montessori identified six such *sensitive periods*:
Sensitivity to order
Sensitivity to language
Sensitivity to walking
Sensitivity to the social aspects of life
Sensitivity to small objects
Sensitivity to learning through the senses.

Sensitivity to order
Sensitivity to order appears in the first year – even in the first month – of life and continues through to the second year. During this time babies and children are striving to sort out and categorize all their experiences, and it is easier for them to do this if there is some kind of order in their lives. They like to be handled in the same way, by the

same person, and in a familiar environment. This should not be confused with an adult's need for neatness; for a baby it is more a need for consistency and familiarity so that he can orientate himself and construct a mental picture of the world. This need is particularly evident in the child from about the age of eighteen months. You may notice that he becomes very upset by changes, such as redecorating his room, moving house or going on vacation.

This coincides with the stage when he first realizes that he is able to manipulate his environment by moving objects from one place to another, but in order to do so he expects to find the objects where he first saw them; if things are different, he will be disorientated.

Sensitivity to language

The ability to use language – to talk – is obviously of major importance as it plays a vital role in all subsequent intellectual growth. The sensitive period for language begins from birth. Your baby hears your voice and watches your lips and tongue – the organs of speech – from birth, absorbing all the time. By the age of six, with almost no direct teaching, he will have acquired a large vocabulary, basic sentence patterns, and the inflections and accent of language. This does not mean that he has achieved full language competence – he will continue to acquire more complex sentence structures and to extend his vocabulary throughout childhood. By six, however, an extraordinary amount has been achieved. If, for any reason, a child is not exposed regularly to language during this period, he will be irrevocably damaged. Depending upon the degree of deprivation, he could suffer more limitations in his intellectual growth than could ever be compensated for totally. Montessori believed, therefore, that it was particularly important for adults to converse with children during this period, continually enriching their language and giving them every opportunity to learn new words.

Sensitivity to walking

When your toddler first learns to walk at around twelve to fifteen months, he has a need to practise and perfect the skill. You walk because you need to get from one place to another, or for exercise, but at this stage your toddler walks for the sake of it. Once he is mobile, he is constantly on the move. In her book, *The Secret of Childhood*, Montessori gives an example of two- and three-year-old children walking for miles and clambering up and down staircases with the sole purpose of perfecting their movements.

We tend to underestimate a child's ability to walk – even very young children are capable of walking long distances, provided they can do it in their own time. There is a difference in going for a walk with a child and taking a child for a walk: it is no use taking a child by the hand and marching along at an adult pace – he will soon become tired and ask to be carried – but if you go at his pace, stopping when he wants to and moving on when he is ready, the walk can be very enjoyable for both of you, and you can cover a surprising amount of ground!

Sensitivity to the social aspects of life

At about the age of two and a half or three, you will notice that your child has become aware that he is part of a group. He begins to show an intense interest in other children of his own age and gradually starts to play with them in a co-operative way. There is a sense of cohesion, which Montessori believed was not instilled by instruction, but which came about spontaneously and was directed by internal drives. She noticed

This parent is going for a walk along the beach with her child, not taking her child for a walk along the beach. The pace is left to the child, who is allowed to stop when she likes, investigate small objects, such as shells and pebbles if she wants to, ask questions and rest for a while if she gets tired.

that at this stage children began to model themselves on adult social behavior and gradually acquire the social norms of their group.

Sensitivity to small objects

At around one, when the child becomes more mobile and therefore has a larger environment to explore, he is drawn to small objects such as insects, pebbles, stones and grass. He will pick something up , look at it closely and perhaps put it in his mouth. The urge to pay attention to detail that children of this age have is part of their effort to build up an understanding of the world.

Identifying different herb smells can develop your child's sense of smell as well as giving her new words of vocabulary. You can even develop it into a game – see page 107.

Sensitivity to learning through the senses

From the moment of his birth, your baby receives impressions of the world around him through his five senses. First the senses of sight and hearing are active, then gradually, as movement develops, the sense of touch plays a role, followed by a sense of taste as he is able to put things into his mouth. Like later child development experts, Maria Montessori recommended that a baby be kept close to the adults caring for him so that he could see and hear everything going on around him. As soon as he can move – crawl or walk – he needs plenty of freedom so that he can explore. This is probably the idea that parents find most difficult to accept, but do try to do so if you can; if you prevent this sensory exploration by constantly saying "no" and confining your baby or toddler in a play pen or strapping him into a chair for long periods of time, it will inhibit his learning.

CHILDREN WANT TO LEARN

Montessori realized that all children have an *inborn motivation* to learn – in fact, you cannot stop them from doing so. It is worth making an effort to understand how best you can foster this, and to develop a positive attitude to the things your child will be expected to learn at different stages of his education, starting from the very earliest days at kindergarten school. All too often a child will say he does not like school or that he does not want to do something that a parent thinks is important to learn about. This sort of attitude can be avoided if you put the Montessori principles into practice right from the start.

It is important to understand what is meant by learning. A simple definition is that it is a process whereby a relatively permanent change of behavior occurs within the individual. One of the great attractions about the Montessori approach is that her ideas, formulated over fifty years ago, have not only stood the test of time, but also much of what she discovered then by keen observation and intuition is now supported by modern research.

It is also important to realize that learning begins *from birth* and that the fundamental processes of how children learn are laid down very early in life. To start with, they learn through play, through experimenting with things in the world around them – for example, the idea that water is wet, that it can be hot or cold, that it can be poured from one container into another, as well as lots of other things, will be learned by your baby or child through playing with water in the bathroom or the kitchen in the normal course of his life.

This spontaneous play is initiated in response to his developmental needs. What you can do to help him is to arrange your home so that it can make available as many different experiences and activities as possible which are appropriate for his age. It is also important that you join in these activities yourself, providing encouragement and social interaction, and also be there to keep an eye on any problem situations that might arise.

All children learn through *active* participation, by being involved in a practical way, and by attempting to do something themselves, particularly by using their *hands*. Montessori put great emphasis on this connection between the brain and movement: Watching the child makes it obvious that the development of his mind comes about through his movements, she felt. She believed the process of learning had three parts: the brain, the senses, and the muscles, and that all three must cooperate for learning to take place.

Recognizing this active approach to learning is important. It is all too easy to make your child sit still and listen or watch while you show him something without letting him join in and participate. Worse still is to sit him in front of the television set where there is no proper interaction at all. He may well spray flour everywhere when he's stirring the cake mixture, or pour water on the floor when he's trying to wash up, but he is going to go on making these mistakes considerably longer if you never give him the opportunity to try to perfect these skills.

All children learn at their own pace and in their own time. No two are alike, so it is never a good idea to force a child to do something against his will. It is much better to introduce an idea and continue to suggest it from time to time until your child shows an interest in it and says he wants to try it – then you can encourage his active participation, building his self-confidence so that

in the future he may come forward more quickly to try something new. The key here is to make the initial activity very simple so that he feels he is succeeding right from the start – to fold a napkin, for instance, is within the capabilities of a child as young as two.

Another aspect of learning Montessori recognized and sympathized with, is a child's need to do things over and over again in order to perfect the actions. When he continually repeats an activity, he is building up automatic patterns which eventually become fixed as mental images. Finally, these mental images can be represented by language; if you talk to your child as much as possible about what he is doing and what is happening to him, he will gradually learn the

Tasks such as napkin-folding can be done even by young children. Carefully matching the edges several times as he lays the table can teach this child about halves and quarters, as well as allowing him to perform a useful function and contribute to family life.

words that correspond to his actions. Research has shown that a child's learning can be considerably enhanced by this interchange of ideas through language between parents and children.

Montessori devised a chart like the one opposite for her student teachers to highlight the connection between the brain and the hands. You can use it to help decide appropriate play and learning materials for the different stages of your child's development.

Learning through play

Many people are confused about the role of play in the Montessori Method: some people seem to think that children in Montessori kindergarten schools simply play all day and don't learn anything; others, who know a little bit more about her theories but have equally misinterpreted them, believe that they are places where children are made to work all the time and are not allowed to play at all.

"Play," of course, can be interpreted in many different ways. When used to refer to an adult activity, it usually means taking part in a game requiring physical or mental skills, or to using a musical instrument. When it is used to refer to a child's activity, however, it is usually taken to mean something that has no serious point to it.

Yet studies of children's play have shown that this is not the case. For the child, play is an enjoyable, voluntary, purposeful and spontaneously chosen activity. It is often creative as well, involving problem solving, learning new social skills, new language and new physical skills. Play is very important to the young child as it helps him to learn new ideas and put them into practice, to adapt socially and to overcome emotional problems, especially in imaginative games such as playing mamas and daddies with dolls.

The misinterpretation of Montessori's ideas has come from two sources. The first is the very rigid way in which some Montessori teachers have insisted on presenting the Montessori materials, leaving no room for discovery or

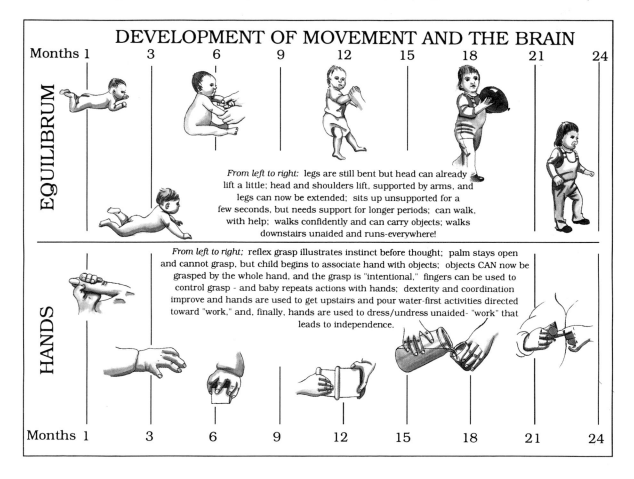

DEVELOPMENT OF MOVEMENT AND THE BRAIN

EQUILIBRUM

From left to right: legs are still bent but head can already lift a little; head and shoulders lift, supported by arms, and legs can now be extended; sits up unsupported for a few seconds, but needs support for longer periods; can walk, with help; walks confidently and can carry objects; walks downstairs unaided and runs-everywhere!

From left to right: reflex grasp illustrates instinct before thought; palm stays open and cannot grasp, but child begins to associate hand with objects; objects CAN now be grasped by the whole hand, and the grasp is "intentional," fingers can be used to control grasp - and baby repeats actions with hands; dexterity and coordination improve and hands are used to get upstairs and pour water-first activities directed toward "work," and, finally, hands are used to dress/undress unaided- "work" that leads to independence.

HANDS

Months 1 3 6 9 12 15 18 21 24

creativity. As parents, you are at an advantage here, since you are not constrained at all by using Montessori equipment and can freely adapt her ideas to your home circumstances.

The second source of misinterpretation has come from Montessori's own writings. She often used the word "work" in relation to children's activities. "Play satisfies only a part of one's nature, work goes deeper and brings satisfaction to one's whole being" she wrote. When she used the word "work" in this context, however, she was not using it in its adult sense – she was applying it to learning.

The activities that children occupy themselves with in a Montessori school may be labeled "work" by the teacher, but they probably look very much like "play" to you. To Montessori the words were synonymous: play is your child's work, simply because it is the means by which he learns.

Throughout her life, Montessori believed in the value of playing games with children. There are many games that can be played with Montessori teaching materials as a way of reinforcing a child's learning – some are included in this book, and they have been selected because they can be played using homemade equipment. Some can be bought commercially.

STAGES OF DEVELOPMENT

Montessori believed that children pass through three distinct phases of development from birth to eighteen, during which they learn qualitatively in different ways. This belief was based on her observations of children, rather than on scientific research, but subsequent findings broadly agree with these ideas, and there is now a lot more in-depth knowledge available.

The age at which they reach a particular stage of development is not rigidly fixed and varies from child to child, but each stage follows the one before and rests firmly on it, and no stage can be omitted. Children often temporarily revert to an earlier stage.

Stage One: Birth to six

From birth to three, the child has what Montessori called an "unconscious" or "absorbent" mind (see page 12). During this time he learns by absorbing impressions from the environment without being aware of the process. Montessori considered this the most important part of the three stages.

From three to six, the child develops a "conscious" mind (see page 12), although he is still absorbing information from his environment, he has now developed a memory and a will. He is also rapidly acquiring language, which makes a significant difference to the way in which he acquires new knowledge.

Stage Two: Six to twelve

Montessori called this period childhood.

Stage Three: Twelve to eighteen

The period is known as adolescence. Montessori believed that so many changes take place during this time that the child needs as much care and attention as he does when he is under the age of six.

We are concerned only with the two parts of Stage One in this book, but it is important to keep all of these stages in mind as your child grows up. Look at him carefully at all times and ask yourself what he likes doing, what he finds easy to do, what he finds difficult and what makes him happiest. Remember that no two children are alike, even within the same family. Each child is unique and will follow his own natural path of development. It is up to you as parents to guide him as he progresses.

ENCOURAGING INDEPENDENCE

From the very beginning, your child will be striving for independence, and the best way to help him achieve it is to show him the skills he needs to succeed. Unfortunately, parents often (from the best of motives) try to help too much, and in the wrong way. Many, for instance, rather

DRESS TO PLEASE

Even small children can learn to put on and take off their own jackets and coats, and in so doing they are beginning to take their first steps on the road to independence. Make this into a game by encouraging them to put on their jackets the Montessori way.

Spread the jacket full out on the floor, the inside facing toward you. Kneel in front of it, then put your arms into the correct armholes.

Using your arms, lift up the whole jacket and whisk it over your head – while still kneeling on the floor.

Push your arms fully into the armholes as the jacket goes over your head, and use your hands to bring the jacket forward to your body as it comes down your back.

The jacket now needs only a few tweaks here and there, and then it's comfortably on, ready for action.

than wait patiently every day while their youngster struggles to do up his buttons, knot his tie or tie his shoe laces, end up doing these things for him. By behaving this way, parents not only put obstacles in the way of the child's natural development, they also prevent the child from carrying out activities that will teach him about the world and help build his self-confidence.

In the kindergarten school, Montessori developed an area of the curriculum she called *Exercises of Practical Life*. These are simple, everyday activities routinely performed by adults to maintain and control the environment in which they live and work. The activities are utilitarian, and so, for the adult, they have a purpose and are a means to an end – and the end result is more important than the process. Practical life activities enable the adult to control his physical and the social environment.

From an early age, every child watches his parents perform these everyday activities and so he has a strong desire to copy and learn from them – it is his way of adapting to the world around him. Unlike an adult, however, performance of these simple daily routines is developmental and absorbing for the child; he is more interested in the processes involved than in the end result.

When "practical life" activities are introduced into kindergarten school classrooms, the behavior of the children changes dramatically. Teachers who introduce activities for the first time cannot believe the difference they make, and how much the child enjoys them. Performance of these simple everyday activities meets the child's need for independence, and because of this, he becomes totally absorbed and concentrated on them. Such exercises develop motor skills and coordination, as well as enriching his vocabulary. Socially, too, new skills are developed as he gradually becomes more aware of other people's needs. The successful completion of tasks which appear to be useful helps to build up his self-esteem and makes him feel worthwhile.

You can involve your child in practical life activities at home – Montessori, in fact, believed that this was a vitally important part of the parents' role. Bear in mind, however, the following Do's and Don'ts as you introduce your child to these activities.

Practical life Do's and Don'ts

- Never give your child *pretend* tools, such as a toy dustpan and brush, or a knife that is blunt and won't really cut, because he will soon discover that he can't make them work, and will become frustrated and give up.

- Provide real tools, making sure that they are the correct size for him.

- When you show him how to do something, do it slowly to give him time to absorb it all, and repeat it several times if necessary to make sure he's got the hang of it.

- If necessary take him through the activity step by step, making sure he understands each step before moving on to the next.

- Let him repeat the activity as many times as he likes; this is how he learns.

It is worth spending a little time each morning thinking about what you plan to do that day and how your child can help you with it. In the chapters that follow you will find many specific suggestions as to how you can help your child to help himself in this way. Where appropriate all of these activities are geared to the different age groups.

Doing up her shoelaces is an activity which involves this child in concentration. She has been shown carefully and slowly how to do it, and then she has been given plenty of time to do it for herself.

USING THE MONTESSORI METHOD

Having identified the universal characteristics of childhood, Maria Montessori then concentrated on how best to implement these discoveries in the bringing up and education of children. To do this, she formulated what is now called the Montessori Method. The main aims are:

- To facilitate the development of the child's unique personality.

- To help him become socially and emotionally well adjusted and grow up as a physically strong and happy child.

- To help make it possible for him to develop to his full intellectual capacity.

DEVELOPING PERSONALITY
There has been considerable research since Montessori's time in the area of personality development, and many of her ideas are consistent with current research.

Montessori viewed each person as an integrated whole and believed that a child constructs or creates his personality through active participation with the environment as he strives for self-actualization. She identified several different stages of development and believed a person's adequacy as an adult depended on his satisfactory progress through each stage.

- During the first stage (infancy), your child needs to be made to feel secure and establish a satisfactory relationship with you, the mother or mother substitute; his physical needs must be met.

- In the next stage, he needs to develop independence. He still needs you, especially when he is trying to do things on his own, because if he fails too often, he will lose confidence and begin to doubt his own ability. Montessori was convinced that by the age of three a child "has already laid down the foundations of his personality" – something most parents would agree with from their own observations of their child as he grows.

- In the final stage lasting from the age of three to six, corresponding with the "conscious" phase of the absorbent mind, your child's personality will be malleable enough to be "normalized," as Montessori put it. This means that with careful and sympathetic handling, he can still come to terms both with himself and the outside world and will appear to be happy and content.

Montessori also believed that children are born with different dispositions and different strengths of character. Some children are strong and some are weak, although neither of these descriptions should be seen as a value judgment – each one has its place.

The chart which appears on the opposite page sets out the many different types of characteristics that appear during the first six years of the child's life.

The parents' role
To help your child's personality develop during his first six years, you need to be aware of the importance of your role in this development, as well as the importance of your attitude toward handling the various situations that arise from day to day. The golden rules are:

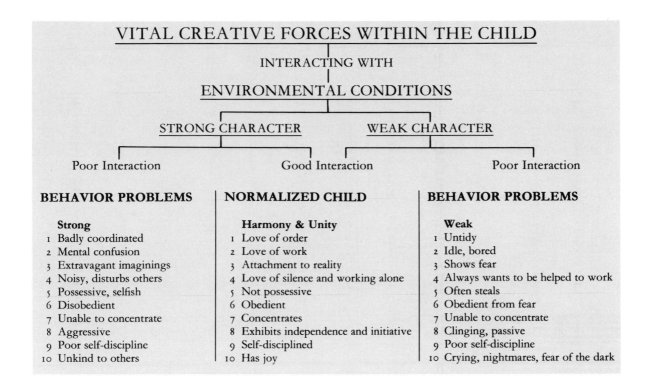

BEHAVIOR PROBLEMS	NORMALIZED CHILD	BEHAVIOR PROBLEMS
Strong	**Harmony & Unity**	**Weak**
1 Badly coordinated	1 Love of order	1 Untidy
2 Mental confusion	2 Love of work	2 Idle, bored
3 Extravagant imaginings	3 Attachment to reality	3 Shows fear
4 Noisy, disturbs others	4 Love of silence and working alone	4 Always wants to be helped to work
5 Possessive, selfish	5 Not possessive	5 Often steals
6 Disobedient	6 Obedient	6 Obedient from fear
7 Unable to concentrate	7 Concentrates	7 Unable to concentrate
8 Aggressive	8 Exhibits independence and initiative	8 Clinging, passive
9 Poor self-discipline	9 Self-disciplined	9 Poor self-discipline
10 Unkind to others	10 Has joy	10 Crying, nightmares, fear of the dark

- To allow freedom within limits

- To respect the individuality of the child

- To resist imposing your own will and personality on your child.

HELPING SOCIAL AND EMOTIONAL ADJUSTMENT

By the age of about six your child should be socially well adjusted, able to behave in an acceptable manner according to the norms of your group. He should be able to cooperate with children of his own age and to have developed a caring and respectful attitude toward other people.

He should by now be showing emotional stability and have a normal attachment to his parents. By this age he shouldn't still need to cling to you and require your constant reinforcement. If he does, it shows that somewhere along the line, he has lost confidence in himself and this needs to be boosted. He should be, instead, quite happy without you if you have given him the necessary reassurance to start with, and when he goes to school, he should be well equipped and ready to cope with new situations as they arise.

Your approach to *discipline* is crucial in this area of development. Montessori wrote a great deal about the importance of encouraging self-discipline in children and the ways she felt this could be brought about. She identified three stages of obedience which lead to self-discipline:

Stage One: Birth to about eighteen months

There is almost no obedience as such, since the child simply does not understand the concept during this stage. However, if your child is treated with consistency and sensitivity, the beginnings of a cooperative relationship will be laid down. The important thing is to meet all your child's needs calmly and lovingly.

Stage Two: About eighteen months to four years

The transition period. Obedience is evident some of the time, depending on how much your child understands. The key to this period is creating a safe environment so that he can explore freely without you constantly having to say "no." Always take time to explain things, so that his understanding grows – temper tantrums can be avoided in this way. He is also in the period when he is sensitive to order, so it is important to establish routines which give him security.

Stage Three: About four to six years

Your child's understanding increases enormously during this time, and by the age of six he should be doing what he is told through this understanding and through his desire to conform. Many parents will have noticed that their children are deeply conservative and don't like to be "different." Of crucial importance at this stage is to give him time to complete activities – try to organize things so that you don't always have to hurry him or stop him from finishing something he has started. This applies equally to a game or to something more basic like washing his hands. You can't expect a child to learn to concentrate if he is always being interrupted halfway through something. The satisfactory completion of a task is an integral part of the Montessori Method; to your child, it is a reward in itself and leads to self-discipline.

Real discipline is not about getting a child to do as he is told, to go to bed at a certain time or to put his toys away. It is about helping him to grow up independently, with a respect for others and control over his own destiny. It is about getting him to care and understand enough about himself so that he can develop self-control.

This can only be brought about in a warm and accepting environment where you respect your child's needs, are tolerant of his feelings and are prepared to give enough time to making sure he has understood why he is expected to behave in a certain way. It is very important to have limits, of course, but limits appropriate to your child's age and level of understanding. In setting them, you need to be sure you really know your child. Ask yourself if your expectations of him are reasonable – are they really within his capabilities? For instance, if he continually fidgets at meal times, are you sure he can really manage on a grown-up chair? If he sits on a pillow, perhaps it slips and makes him feel insecure. Maybe you should get him a booster seat for a while so that he can reach the table comfortably.

The important point is to adopt a positive approach. If you are constantly being negative, he will soon pick up the message that he can never achieve your approval, and he will soon give up trying, making the situation even worse. Don't expect him to be perfect – no one is – so try not to be too critical. If you adopt an encouraging attitude, he will gradually learn what is expected of him and will want to do it because he is naturally keen to please you.

It is unfair to expect your child to do something you are not prepared to do yourself. Once again table manners are often an area of conflict: you may tell your child to sit up at meal times or perhaps not to bring toys or books to the table, yet look at yourself critically and ask yourself how often you yourself rest your elbows on the table, tip your chair or read the newspaper during a meal! This means making an effort to set rules or guidelines which are fair, and to communicate them properly to your child, explaining exactly what is wanted and, if he's old enough to understand, why. Last, but not least, always try to be consistent in your expectations – if a child is always breaking a rule, then it is probably because the rule is inappropriate.

Always try to create a safe environment for your child, where she can explore freely – this is how she learns. Explain to her (as this mother is doing) why she should protect herself against the sun rather than just ordering her to do so.

Playing with other children helps to develop social skills. It can also encourage learning and develop concentration, too, especially when the play is as engrossing as it is in this sand box.

One final point: Maria Montessori's view of reward and punishment has a bearing on her philosophy of fostering appropriate self-discipline in a child. She believed that children should not be rewarded with presents even if they were doing the right thing, because it would encourage them to carry on doing the activity for the sake of the reward rather than for the pleasure of the activity itself. She saw punishment as a vicious circle – a child who is constantly punished becomes so frightened of doing something wrong that his brain becomes muddled and confused; and, as a result, he will do it wrong again, which will lead to more punishment. . .

Your role in the socialization process

● Don't be *over-possessive* or over-protective toward your child, as this will hinder his innate desire to explore and discover by him-self. An over-protected child is over-anxious and shows less originality than his friends.

● Don't make *excessive demands* on your child's affections – let him come to you when he needs affection. This is not to say you should lack warmth toward him, or be *rejecting* in any way. If you are, he may show an excessive desire for approval or affection from other adults, such as teachers. Because he may be lacking in confidence, he may behave impassively and not develop the ability to concentrate well.

● Don't lay down the law in an authoritarian way – this could cause your child to become either timid or nonassertive, while giving the appearance of being obedient and polite. This isn't real obedience, doing what is right because he knows it is best; it is passive acquiescence – doing what he is told to avoid a scene. He will become either unnaturally inhibited and withdrawn or the opposite – rebelling against the constant nagging and becoming aggressive and unruly. There is nothing worse than telling a child to do something "because I say so." This leads to justifiable resentment, and a bright four to six year old will soon learn to answer back, building up an unfortunate vicious circle of confrontations between you and him.

- Don't be too easygoing. Being *over-permissive* produces a child who tends to show swings of mood from confidence to lack of it and who develops little or no self-control. Try to be democratic, involving your child in decision-making and allowing him freedom to express his ideas while being quite clear about how far you are prepared to go. If you encourage him to develop critical skills while maintaining a sensible approach to safety, you will find he will be well-adjusted and happy.

YOUR ROLE IN DEVELOPING YOUR CHILD'S INTELLECTUAL CAPACITY

A general definition of what is meant by intelligence is that it is the capacity to learn new skills and to be able to use them to adapt to the environment and the culture in which people live. Because different cultures value different skills, there are different views of intelligence. Furthermore, there are thought to be different types of intelligence. The ability to acquire knowledge and learn facts is one, the ability to solve problems is another, and the ability to use the information acquired in a creative way is a third.

Awareness of all of these different aspects of intelligence will help you to understand what is happening to your child when you find that, as a three year old, he is having more difficulty in holding a pencil and drawing a picture than his best friend. You may find he is better able to count or has a better sense of musical rhythm at the same age. All children are different, and they should all be given the opportunity to develop their different intellectual abilities in their own time without pressure from their parents.

Montessori emphasized several important ways in which adults help children to develop to their full intellectual potential, and these can be summed up in the following way:

- Allow your child to be active, enabling him to learn through sensory exploration of the world around him.

- Recognize the sensitive periods (see page 13) and allow him to repeat an activity until he has perfected it.

- Recognize the importance of motivation and how it affects learning.

A child *wants to learn*. There is no need to do something to motivate him, such as offer him candy if he learns his two times tables. With enough encouragement from you, his inborn motivation to learn will appear. Left to himself, a child will spontaneously choose to do something that interests him. Unfortunately, some children lose this inborn motivation because their natural curiosity has been frustrated. Children like this often have difficulty in settling at school. Although a good teacher will make an effort to find ways of remotivating such children, occasionally they cannot, and a long-term resistance to school can build up.

The implication for you as parents is that, as with discipline, it is best not to try and impose your will on your child. You may think you know what is best for him to play with, but is it really true? Perhaps your child is busy taking pans out of the kitchen cupboard. He may be making rather a lot of noise, and you may wonder why he won't play with the expensive construction toy you bought him. Surely, you say to yourself, it is more educational? Yet if you look at what he is doing in the cupboard, he may in fact be involved in a lot of hidden learning. He could be piling up the saucepans, for instance, and this involves sorting, which is an important element in early maths, or he may be putting things into them and taking them out again learning about volume – another element of early mathematics. He doesn't know he's doing this, of course, but if you take the trouble to sit with him and suggest new ways of sorting those saucepans, or fitting the right lids onto each one, you are probably helping his intellectual development just as much as if you had helped him make a tower with his Lego. If you remove him from the saucepan cupboard just when he is really involved, there will almost certainly be tears and anger – and, in a way, can you blame him?

● **Encourage independent learning** One of the many benefits of the Montessori approach is that the child becomes an independent learner. The way to encourage this is to allow your child to do the activities he likes most, to encourage him to complete them and then let him discover for himself his mistakes. The temptation for a parent is to interfere and tell the child that he has made a mistake. If you can learn to wait, more often than not, he will discover for himself how to get it right. In the Montessori classroom, the didactic materials often have what is referred to as a "control of error" built in, which means that there is something about the materials that gives the child a clue to the correct way of doing the activity.

You can do this at home. If you want your child to set the table correctly, for instance, make sure that he has the correct number of knives and forks to start with, so that when he has finished, if he has one too few knives, he knows he must have doubled up somewhere and he can go back and check by himself to see where the missing knife

has gone – there is no need for you to say "You've got it wrong!" He will get used to getting things right by himself and become an independent learner.

● **Modeling** Recognize that your child will acquire a large part of his learning through watching and imitating adults and other children, a type of learning sometimes known as modeling.

If you are aware of this aspect of learning, it will help you to consider carefully the way you behave in front of your child. For example, a child who observes a parent being aggressive may think this is normal and that it's all right for him to be aggressive, too. On the other hand, if he is brought up by a parent who is always gentle and friendly, he is likely to copy this behavior and unconsciously try to imitate it. Bear this in mind when showing your child how to do something new; always try to do things very slowly and carefully so that he can easily copy you and, through trying it out for himself, eventually learn a new skill.

● **Help your child to learn things step by step** While working with children with special needs, Montessori observed that it was easier for them to learn if she taught them one thing at a time and made sure they had accomplished this first before moving on to the next stage. She tried this approach with normal children and found that it worked with them, too. It may seem obvious when written here, but when you are showing your child something new, be sure that you do not go too quickly for him, and that each of the "steps" are small enough for him to handle comfortably. Teach him this way, and he will probably succeed.

Helping to prepare for a meal by taking part in setting the table is an enjoyable activity for your child. What is more, it provides another opportunity for active learning, since it includes activities such as sorting silverware and pouring water from one container into another.

AGES AND STAGES

2

STAGE AND DEVELOPMENT

Unconscious Absorbent Mind: Physical Growth/Skills
● balance, physical control and mobility increase considerably
● climbs up and down stairs ● reads everything in sight ●
learns to run and jump ● pushes, pulls and lifts objects and
toys in environment ● learns to kick, throw, and catch a ball ●
awareness of self in relation to space ● fine motor skills
develop and change; now begins to manipulate small objects ●
hand-eye coordination develops

Emotional and Social
● develops sense of self ● begins to develop idea of sex roles –
reinforced by parent reactions ● fear of strangers and
separation – often quite marked at this age

Intellectual
● nerve connections in brain reach peak; those that are used
survive ● learning through senses; sight and hearing improve
considerably ● keen observation of small objects (sensitive
period) ● tends to attribute life to inanimate objects and
human attributes to animals, eg talks to them like human
beings ● thinking skills develop; child begins to use symbols ●
fantasy play rich during this period ● memory and attention;
steady improvement in long- and short-term memory ● ability
to concentrate for longer periods

Language
● names objects ● obeys commands ● understands much

Words
● 200/300 productive speech

3

STAGE AND DEVELOPMENT

Conscious Absorbent Mind: Physical Growth/Skills
● physical abilities undergo steady progress ● walks and runs
with confidence ● becomes physically daring, climbs anything
● fine motor skills; drawings begin to include recognizable
shapes

Emotional and Social
● self concept still being formed and influenced by reaction of
others ● describes himself in physical terms – color of hair, etc
● begins to make friends; centered on shared play things ●
attachment behavior strong in strange situations ● desire for

independence ● emotional stability depends on quality of
relationship with adults

Intellectual
● imagination vivid ● concepts become more complex as they
construct picture of world ● strong desire to investigate
things ● gradual increase in short-term memory; can
remember 3 digits ● begins to identify events in past and
future

Language
● rapid increase in language ● incessantly asks questions

Words
● 1000 productive speech

4

STAGE AND DEVELOPMENT

Physical Growth/Skills
● very active, enjoys gymnastics, can control his movements
and responds to adult direction ● begins to walk up and down
stairs using alternate feet ● fine motor skills developing; draws
what knows – not what sees ● can draw shapes; writing
begins to have more control

Emotional and Social
● sex role; prefers to play with friend of same sex ● friendship
plays a stronger, more important role; children distinguish
between what others do and they do, and they begin to make
choices about who they play with ● social skills now quite

developed and confident children leave parents to go to
school or other people's houses without problems

Intellectual
● understanding concepts is increasingly being affected by the
use of symbols, mental images and languages; more aware of
wider world around, eg neighborhood ● fantasies and stories
must be carefully controlled ● stories based on reality help
children of this age to sort out fact and fiction

Language
● speech grammatically correct ● counts up to 20 ● begins to
read and write

Words
● 1500 productive speech

5

STAGE AND DEVELOPMENT

Physical Growth/Skills
● has developed poise and control and is no longer restless
and constantly moving ● playing physical games is enjoyed
and social content important ● riding a bicycle and roller
skating where coordination and skills are involved, enjoyed ●
fine motor control now good – enjoying counting and
drawing, and playing games that involve fine motor skills;
building construction toys ● drawing and writing continue to
become more refined

Emotional and Social
● sex role; most children develop stereotypical views of
acceptable behavior of male and female ● friendships become

more stable; personalities and interests are involved in the
choice they make about friends ● conscience develops;
children understand and follow rules

Intellectual
● growing understanding of relationships in the world and
around them ● begins to understand quite complex processes
such as where food comes from ● developing reading,
writing, and number skills ● aided by structure and multi-
sensory approach

Language
●fluent speech ● reads and writes

Words
● 2000 productive speech

● **Help your child develop concentration** If you can help your child develop concentration at an early age, you will be giving him a skill that will stand him in good stead when he goes to school. The way Montessori recommends that you develop his concentration is by always making sure that any activity you give him to do is appropriate for his age and capability. Children lose interest when things are either too difficult or too easy.

● **Encourage a positive attitude to learning** If you have a positive attitude toward your child when he is trying to learn something, he will be encouraged and, in his turn, he will be positive, too.

● **Help him develop memory skills** It is thought that there are several kinds of memory: some children are able to learn by rote more easily than others; some appear to have good visual memory; others appear to have good auditory memory, while yet others have a good memory for movement. Montessori devised several games to help visual and auditory memory, and some are included later in this book. They will give your child practice in particular skills, and as they will do so within the context of games, it will be especially enjoyable for him.

● **Encourage language development** Montessori wrote a great deal about the importance of language development during the first six years of life – while he is in a sensitive period – and research since her time has drawn attention to the relationship between language and learning, and language and thought. She was the forerunner of one important theory that maintains that the child is born with a natural capacity for language and communication because we, as human beings, possess inborn structures that enable us to make sense of the sounds and words we hear.

It isn't difficult to see why you should be aware of the importance of language development and its connection with intelligence. From early on – even before speech is developed – communication between your baby and you is child-driven. He likes to hear your voice, watch your face and focus on your eyes right from the moment of birth, and his response is to smile. Yours is to talk more, so that he smiles more, and so the process continues.

The more you engage in language activities with your child the better. Talking to him, giving him instructions, telling him stories, reading to him and, of course, listening to him are all important.

As a parent you will be called upon to play many roles in your child's life. First and foremost, you must create a loving environment so that your child grows up forming intimate relationships within the family group. This gives a sound foundation and enables him to form meaningful and lasting relationships with others outside the family.

You must also provide the daily care to make sure he has a healthy and safe life. Another role is to help your child construct his unique personality – you must be flexible enough not to impose your own personality and will upon him. Yet another is to encourage the development of independence, to allow freedom within clearly defined limits and to promote the child's good self-image and feeling of security.

You should also create a stimulating environment to bring about early learning, which begins from the moment of birth and occurs most easily during the early years, help your child build an inner life which is rich and rewarding, and, last but not least, help him assimilate his own culture and develop respect for others. The chart opposite will help you trace and pace all of this development.

Maria Montessori placed a great deal of emphasis on the child's absorbent mind – she believed the first six years to be absolutely the most vital period in the child's development. The role of parents is not to be underestimated.

Planning Your Home Around Your Child

INTRODUCTION

From what we have already discussed about Montessori's approach to child rearing practices and education during the first six years of life, we know that she placed great emphasis on three central ideas.

- First and foremost, she believed that there should be as much physical and intellectual freedom for the child as possible.

- Second, she believed the environment itself, and the way it is prepared, has a profound influence on development and learning.

- Third, she believed that the way the child is treated by the adults around her, particularly her parents, has a profound effect upon her development.

HOME ENVIRONMENT

It is a central role for you as parents to prepare your home for your child, so that all of these ideas can become practical possibilities. To do this, first of all look at your home from her point of view. She is, after all, part of the family, and she should be made to feel that she has an important place in it. There are six basic principles to keep in mind as you plan your home around your child.

Child-sized In a Montessori classroom, everything is child-sized. This is because it is literally as Montessori called it, the *Casa dei Bambini* or Children's House, and, except for the teachers, it is used only by children. Home is different, of course, because it will be shared by all the family, but it is possible to introduce furniture of the right scale into various rooms. The child's bedroom, for instance, is probably going to be used entirely by her, so this room at least can be

prepared with everything child-sized. There will be other rooms, too, where the child, depending on her age, will be able to participate and have a place for things of her own – the chapters that follow make specific suggestions.

Close proximity As we saw earlier, the child starts learning from the moment she is born and, what is more, most of what he learns about the world, her culture, language, and heritage is through her parents. So if it is at all possible, try to arrange your life so that your child can spend most of her time near to you or her mother substitute – father, nanny, grandparents, babysitter. Even a young baby who cannot yet sit up should be near where the action takes place, close to the mother during waking hours, where she can observe, hear and learn about the daily happenings of her household.

Freedom within limits A child learns by being active, by touching things, tasting them, smelling them, listening to them and looking at them intently. When she is restrained excessively by being strapped with reins or in a playpen, her horizons are being limited. Although, obviously, care must be taken to make sure of her safety until she has learned about the dangers of her environment, the only other limits to her freedom that should be considered are those activities and behaviors mutually agreed by the family as not being allowed.

If you institute a rule, but then find it is constantly being broken, observe your child and try to understand why it isn't working – there is probably something wrong with the rule, not with the child. Perhaps the rule needs changing or modifying to be more appropriate for the age of the child.

Involve your child in family life If a child is always banished to her own "play room," or told to go and find something to do until you have finished what you are doing, she will not be able to learn so quickly how to function within a group and how to control her own environment and become independent. It is through watching, helping and participating in daily activities, such as making the beds, washing the dishes, shopping, cooking and eating meals as part of the family, that your child will learn these fundamental things.

Meeting your child's needs Prepare the environment to meet the child's needs; they should include not only the physical, but also the psychological. As mentioned before, the child constructs her unique personality by interaction with the environment, and to do this in the best possible way, her needs must be met. Her physical needs are readily identifiable – food,

clothing, shelter and safety, plus enough space to move around in – but she has psychological needs, too, and these include love, social acceptance and respect for her as a human being.

By providing all of these things for her, you will help her develop self-respect. Since she is, in her first six years of life, striving to be part of her cultural group, too, she also needs to learn about and identify with her own culture.

Positive discipline It is much better to teach your child to do things the right way rather than concentrate on correcting her when she does them the wrong way. If necessary, be prepared to show her how to do something over and over again until you are sure she understands what is needed. Try to help her develop self-discipline by example, encouragement and reason.

With these six basic principles in mind, let us look at each room in the house with your child and her needs in mind.

This elegant room was NOT designed with this child in mind – it says, "Don't touch! It's not for you!" Adapting a room like this so that your child can feel at ease and function in it is surprisingly easy, as the chapters that follow make clear.

YOUR CHILD'S BEDROOM

Of all the rooms in the house, this is the one that your child can truly call her own. Even if she is sharing it with a sibling, they can have areas which are exclusively theirs. This is where you can really put the Montessori principles into practice, where everything can be child-sized. On the other hand, unless you know you are quite definitely going to be moving before she is about six, you need to think ahead a bit so that your growing child's changing size and tastes are catered for, since you obviously don't want to be completely refurnishing her room every two years!

BEDS
Montessori recommended that young babies should sleep on a mattress on the floor so that they could get up easily when their sleep and rest was over. Even though most modern babies sleep in cribs, when it comes to changing to a bed, it is a very good idea to get a low level one so that your toddler can easily get in and out by herself. There is also less likelihood of bumps if she falls out, which children who have been used to sleeping in a crib sometimes do to start with.

Either a low divan or a Japanese futon would be suitable. A futon is a good idea if space is limited, as it can be folded away to provide floor space for play.

It's also a good idea to provide your child with a comforter quilt instead of blankets and sheets. It is much easier for her to make her own bed if she has a quilt, and she can be taught to do this, as a matter of course, from a very early age.

Practical life activity
To encourage your child to make her own bed, make a game of shaking out the comforter. Stand

(Left) In his bedroom, this child has his own special shelves he can reach, where he can display his favorite things – like models of dinosaurs! (Right) This particular bedroom also has a child-sized desk where this little boy can draw or paint, or perhaps practice writing his alphabet. Beside him are reachable shelves where he can store his books.

her on one side of the bed while you are at the other. Get her to hold the two corners at her end, while you hold the other two at yours and then shake the quilt up and down so that it makes waves over the bed. When you've finished the game, you can help her put the quilt back on the bed. As she gets bigger, you can gradually persuade her to straighten her bed herself.

CLOTHES STORAGE

Closets and drawers should be child-sized, allowing easy access to take things out and, more important, to put them away again! Put sturdy, blunt-ended hooks on the back of the door for the clothes to hang – make them easy to reach, but at different heights so that longer items don't trail on the floor. You could also put a low level rod in a closet, at child height, for small coathangers.

Drawers should slide easily, but make sure there is a "stop" on them so that they aren't constantly pulled right out and emptied all over the floor. If possible, label them with pictures of the different kinds of clothes kept in each one, with the relevant words as well. Your child will soon tell you if a stray pair of socks has wandered into the sweater drawer.

When you have done a batch of washing and ironing, separate your child's clothes from the others and suggest that she sorts them into piles on her bed. She can either sort them into types of clothes (socks, underpants, sweaters, shirts, etc.), into matching colors, or even into textures or materials. Then she can put them away in the correct drawers or closet. An older child could try to guess which pile has the most items, then count them to see whether she is right. (This helps judgment: after all, six T-shirts look a lot less in a pile than three pairs of winter pajamas.)

TOY STORAGE

If your child is going to spend quite a lot of time playing in her bedroom, it is a good idea to put up some low level shelves for her toys so that she can reach them easily and attempt to keep them neat.

Provide storage boxes for small items such as construction toys, farm animals, model cars, etc. You can buy special plastic stacking boxes in different colors. Again, it is a good idea to label them, either with pictures or words, or preferably both. One large toy box is not a good idea because it encourages disorder, and your child will soon stop caring for her toys because they are always jumbled up and messy.

Make sure there is shelf space for books – even a baby should have simple picture books around her. Some people like to display large format picture books face forward, rather than spine out. They are more appealing that way, and your child is more likely to pick them up when she is attracted to the picture on the cover.

OTHER FURNITURE

If you want your child to draw and paint, or do other craft-based activities in her bedroom, make sure she has a low table with decent work space plus more than one low chair, so that she can play with friends. If it doesn't have a plastic surface, then cover it with washable oilcloth. You may want to think about the floor covering, too – although carpets are warmest, if she is likely to play regularly in her room, it might be better to have something that is easily washable, such as sealed cork tiles.

It is also a good idea to leave some wall space for displaying pictures and timelines (see page 69). You can put up cork tiles so that such items can be pinned to the wall and changed regularly. Or make a large, felt-covered bulletin board in a simple frame and hang it on the wall like a picture.

Practical life activity

When you've been working on some messy activity with your child, why not get her to help clean up? Afterward, once everything has been put away, she can use a cloth to wipe her table, and, depending on the surface, she can use a mop or cloth to clean the floor.

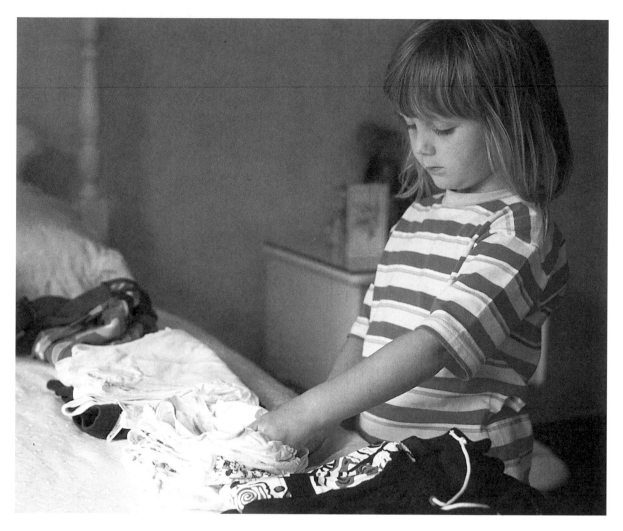

DECORATION

This is your child's room, so above all it should be an inviting and pleasant place for her to be in. The atmosphere should be attractive, and when your child is old enough, she should be involved in helping to choose the furnishings. Light pastel colors are appropriate, as it is not a good idea to overstimulate a child by having wallpaper that is too bright or busy, and it is sensible to use washable paint and vinyl wallpaper. Providing a blackboard, or simply painting an area of the wall with blackboard paint (available at craft shops) would also allow free expression for the budding artist or for when she begins to write.

Children love to help their parents with tasks around the house. Here, this little girl helps her mother by folding and putting away her own clothes. Notice how meticulously she is doing it.

Safety is at all times of paramount importance. It is good for your child to be able to look out of the window safely, so put in safety catches that allow it to open, but not enough for her to climb out. Never fit bars — with modern fitments it should never be necessary to resort to prison-like devices, no matter how high up you live. Accessible electric plugs should also have safety devices attached to them.

THE LIVING ROOM

The living room is shared by all the family, so it is perhaps the best room in which to establish respect for everyone. Usually parents like to keep this room presentable for their own peace of mind and in case visitors unexpectedly drop in, but at the same time it should have an atmosphere of warmth, comfort and relaxation. Many people try to banish their children from it, rationalizing that if the children have their own playroom or bedroom, there should be no need to "clutter up" the adult living room with toys.

This is quite contrary to Montessori's philosophy, however. In her view, children have equal status within the family and shouldn't be excluded from any area in the home. As she continually stressed, a child learns so much simply by being with her parents and watching what they are doing.

So, if at all possible, provide a place in the living room where your child can keep some of her things, such as books and toys. A cupboard may be the best compromise as toys can then simply be shut away at the end of the day. Perhaps she could also have her own low chair or floor pillow to sit on, and a sturdy coffee table (*not* glass-topped) is an ideal height for a child to work on. This way she will be made to feel she has a place in the living room, too. Of course, you can encourage her to keep her corner neat.

Practical life activities
Allow your child to decide what she wants to keep in her special closet and arrange it with her so that everything is easy to reach. It is difficult to teach a child to be neat if every time she wants to play with a particular jigsaw she has to tip her Lego on the floor first because the puzzle is underneath it! Limit the toys that she keeps there; and if you're going to allow drawing and coloring, avoid felt-tipped pens as the ink is often indelible and could permanently stain carpets or upholstery. Provide colored pencils or wax crayons instead.

Encourage your child to put one thing away before starting on a different activity. You can't expect this to happen every time – it's particularly difficult when she has friends to play – but be especially encouraging when she does it spontaneously. One way of encouraging her to clear up her things is to do yours at the same time, and see who finishes first.

ELECTRICAL EQUIPMENT
You can also teach her early how to respect the furniture and things belonging to adults. For example, you may not wish her to use the expensive music center or video until she has learned to do it properly. It is surprising how quickly very young children learn to use video cassette players – they don't need to know why they work, just the way they do. . . . They probably need to be supervised the first few times, so that they know which way the cassette goes in, and that poking your fingers into any electrical equipment is dangerous, but by two and a half or three, most children are quite adept at using such machines.

With any sort of electrical equipment – lamps, television, CD players or whatever – the cords should never trail over the floor where anyone, child or adult, can trip over them. Unused electric sockets should be protected with safety devices if children use the room a lot.

This young child has been taught the necessary social and language skills for answering the telephone. It also builds her self-esteem as she realizes she can participate and perform a useful and helpful task.

Practical life activities (Age 2½ up)

Start your child off with a simple cassette player. Let her have her own tapes to listen to – there are some excellent kindergarden rhymes and story tapes on the market. Teach her how to put them in the machine and take them out carefully. Give her her own special tape box, and color-code it with stickers so that she can keep the tapes in order. An older child could learn to store them alphabetically if you provide clear letter dividers.

TAKING CARE

You should teach your child not to jump on sofas and chairs. You probably won't want her to eat off the carpet in your living room either. She will soon get used to the idea that eating is something that is done in the kitchen or dining room as a matter of course. Children will take their lead from you. If you do allow the occasional drink and cake in the living room, perhaps while you are having a cup of coffee or tea yourself, you could bring her chair up to the low table and let her have her snack there as well. If you are worried about the possibility of spills, you can protect your carpets and upholstery from damaging accidents by spraying them with a stain-resistant coating.

You might feel that you have to put breakable ornaments and valuable equipment out of reach, but this is neither necessary nor always desirable. Your child will be more curious about what she is not allowed to have if they are kept mysteriously out of reach. Allow her to handle things carefully, using both hands. Explain that ornaments are pretty things to look at, and show her that you don't pick them up all the time, but that you look at them.

It is all a matter of time persuading your child to use things for the purpose for which they are designed. Respect is taught by example. Always show your child respect, and she will learn to respect you and the things you ask her to do.

(Left) Spending time together as a family is particularly important when your children are growing up, and the living room is usually the best "family activity" room in the house. (Right) This child has her own place in this family living room: a seat that is an appropriate height, and low-level drawers where she can keep her own tapes and other toys.

Practical life activities

To help teach your child to take care of objects in the living room, let her help with the dusting and polishing. Give her her own dusting cloth and show her how to take items off the shelves individually and dust them carefully, putting them back in the same place. You'll probably find she is a lot more thorough than you are, although a lot slower. Help her to feel the different textures of the various ornaments – glass, china, wood and so on, and get her to talk about whether they are warm or cold, and why she thinks they might feel that way.

- If she has her own place to sit at the coffee table or other occasional table, let her help with polishing them, too. Children love to see the difference as the dullness of the unpolished area gives way to a clean, smooth, shiny new surface. You'll probably find that she spends quite a long time on one small area – this is excellent, since it means it's improving her concentration.

- If she has spilled some crumbs on the carpet, rather than being cross with her (remember she may be too young to eat a piece of cake without making crumbs), let her help clean them up by herself. She can use a stiff brush and dustpan – although she probably won't manage to do it very well at first, she will enjoy the practice and will master it after a few attempts.

THE KITCHEN

Ordinary kitchens are obviously designed for adult use, and you may have had yours installed long before your first child came along. But for many families with young children, the kitchen becomes one of the most important rooms in the house, the one where everyone tends to congregate. When your children are small, it is particularly important that they should be accommodated there, because you will spend a lot of time preparing, eating and clearing up after meals, and your children will want to be near you while you are doing it.

Kitchens are also designed to be easy to clean – they usually have washable surfaces. Many families do not have an area in the house that can be designated entirely for play activities such as art and craft, and, obviously, the kitchen is the best place for these "messy" activities.

There is usually lots of storage space, so one of the kitchen cupboards can be used for storing the materials. Make sure they are within easy reach so that your child can take out and put things away by herself.

Even more important is to allow children to join in all the activities that the kitchen is normally used for. Simple adjustments may have to be made to enable your child to share in some of them, but there are so many ways in which she can benefit from joining in your daily activities in the kitchen that it is well worth the effort involved in organizing it. Preparing food and cooking it, washing dishes, loading the dishwasher, helping load the washing machine and tumble dryer, for instance, can all provide a whole education in themselves!

Here, a child helps to load the dishwasher, and in so doing learns to sort dishes and silverware into categories and how to handle sharp objects like knives and forks.

SAFETY FIRST

Most accidents occur in the home and especially in the kitchen, so take these sensible precautions:

- Protect your child from scalding and burns by turning all saucepan handles inward. You can fit guard rails around burners, but they can be more of a hindrance than a help.

- Make sure the controls for your burners are on top of the stove and not on the front, so that they cannot be turned on too easily by small inquisitive fingers.

- Teach your children as early as possible that stoves and ovens are HOT. A ceramic stovetop is not the best thing for a family with young children, because they remain hot even though they don't look it, and a child may not notice a warning light.

- Make sure all electric cooking utensils are stored out of reach and are only used with supervision.

- Use coiled cords on your electric countertop appliances so that they do not trail over the edge of the counter.

- Never leave a child alone in the kitchen when you've got something cooking on the stove. If someone comes to the door, take your child with you.

- Keep all dangerous detergents, bleaches, etc., in a cupboard that is either kept locked or is out of reach.

Participating in the daily activity of washing dishes provides this mother and child with an opportunity to do something together. The concentration level is high as he carefully lays the clean plate on the draining board. During such simple activities, he can learn many new words and concepts, as many questions are asked and answered.

Practical life activities

The kitchen is full of opportunities for practical life activities and positive learning experiences. Try not to discourage your child's curiosity – find the time to let her help you. If the temptation is to send her off to sit in front of the television because you are busy cooking something complicated for eight guests who are arriving in half an hour, then try to resist it! Try to find her a child-sized task to do, something you know will keep her absorbed while you get on with what you are doing.

WASHING THE DISHES

Make sure you have a sturdy step which brings her up to the height of the sink, show her how to roll up her sleeves and put on her own waterproof apron, and then show her how to fill the bowl with soapy water, give her a cloth or a brush and let her wash your equipment.

Involve her in this activity as early as possible. She will handle the breakable plates and glasses with great care if you spend enough time showing her what to do. Remember that even while undertaking such a modest task as washing dishes she is learning a tremendous amount. Her maths, for instance, will benefit because she is learning about volume, shape and size, and you could help explain such ideas as full, half-full, more, less, too much, not enough and so on. There are also scientific principles involved in how water and soap affect substances such as grease.

Loading the dishwasher

Show her how to load the dishwasher, if you have one. She will be learning about shape and the relationship between different sizes of plates, cups, and silverware. Get her to help you unload it, too, so that she learns where different things go in the kitchen. If any dishes live in high cupboards teach her to get her own step and let her put the things away, a few items at a time, by herself.

HELPFUL HINTS

- Provide your child with a sturdy stepstool on which to stand so she is the right height for the sink or counter. Keep it in its own space in a cupboard so that she learns to get it out and put it away as a matter of course.

- Put the dishes that are used most often for family meals in a low level cupboard so your child can easily reach them.

- Provide lots of wooden spoons, sturdy plastic mixing bowls and spatulas for cooking.

- Make sure you have good-sized see-through measuring cups and metal or plastic measuring spoons.

- Provide your child with her own waterproof apron, and hang it on a hook which she can easily reach. She will soon learn to put it on as a matter of course. A washable plastic one which goes over her head and preferably has sleeves gives the best protection.

SETTING THE TABLE

If plates needed for setting the table are kept in a low cupboard and silverware is in a drawer that can be easily reached, when it is time to set the table she should be able to do it by herself. Starting with family meals in the kitchen, you'll soon be able to progress to more formal table setting in the dining room.

Table setting is a good way to teach your child the difference between left and right, and it will also appeal to her sensitivity to order. Children positively enjoy making sure that mats, silverware, dishes, and condiments are neatly arranged on the table. She may not get it right immediately, but with plenty of praise and reinforcement for her first efforts, you'll soon find it is done perfectly every time, even by a three year old.

COOKING

As good chefs will tell you, cooking is both an art and a science, so involve your child in it as much as possible – cooking with a young child is one of the most rewarding and educational experiences in the home.

It is easy to find some part of a recipe that can be done by a two year old, and older children are capable of cooking dishes and even simple meals from start to finish by themselves. Simply measuring the ingredients is a major step in scientific experience. She can learn the difference between weight (of dry ingredients) and volume (of wet *and* dry if you work in cup measurements), and you can teach her the various names of the units of measurement such as ounces, pounds, pints, quarts, and gallons. Let her measure out the ingredients for you – put the measuring cup on the table at her eye level so she can see the calibrations exactly.

Five and six year olds can start to work out how much more of an ingredient they will need to add to reach the correct amount, if you put about half or a third of the amount in first. You can also start them on subtraction, by putting too much in and asking them to remove enough to correct it. If an older child wishes to cook using a recipe, ask her to read it through first and to follow the instructions carefully. This is an important step toward learning how to do scientific experiments, which require this step-by-step attention to detail.

Make sure she has developed the skills needed, such as mixing, stirring or cutting, before letting her embark on the project. Show her all the stages involved, and let her see the end product before she starts (many cookbooks now provide illustrations of finished dishes next to their recipes). Although anything involving knives and heat needs constant supervision, if you take it slowly, even quite young children can learn to manipulate knives safely and to treat hot ovens and pans with great respect.

Provide your child with her own oven mitts – if you're handy with a needle, you can make her her own small pair which will be less likely to slip off than large adult ones. Hang them on a hook near the stove at her height and make sure she puts them back each time so you always know where to find them.

CLEANING AND WASHING

There is no reason why your child shouldn't help to sort out the clothes for the washing machine. Teach her to distinguish between brightly colored or dark clothes that need a low temperature wash, woolens and delicate fabrics, and robust whites for the hot wash. This provides a good opportunity to learn to identify colors by name and to find out where the different fabrics come from – whether they are man-made or natural, or from animals or plants. Older children can also learn to read the symbols on the labels of clothes so that they know which type of wash to use for them.

Whether you use a tumble dryer or hang the washing outside, there is a good opportunity for sorting games when the clothes are dry. Sheets, pillowcases and comforter quilt covers can be folded and put away into their separate drawers or shelves, and socks can be sorted into pairs. Your six year old could even be shown how to iron simple garments such as T-shirts, or dishcloths and pillowcases. Adjust the ironing board down to her level and keep an eye on her to avoid burns.

At an early age, too, your child can help with clearing up, wiping the table, sweeping the floor, and cleaning pots and pans. Provided you involve her in activities that are appropriate, and within her capabilities, and that you have the right attitude (which is positive and enjoyable), all your activities together will be rewarding for both of you and will help to build a good relationship between you.

Learning to cook can provide an early introduction to both mathematics and science, as the child begins to understand weights and measurements, and the effects of beating ingredients, mixing solids and liquids, and heating mixtures.

THE BATHROOM

This is another room your child will use frequently, and she should be encouraged to become independent here as early as possible. To do this, show her how to turn the faucet on and off, how to use the plugs in the bath and the wash basin, and how to turn the shower on and off.

If you are having a new shower installed, the single-lever type of "On-Off" control is best for children to use by themselves – make sure that it is at child height and show her where to point the temperature arrow so that she does not scald herself when she turns on the water. If you have separate hot and cold water faucets, show her how to put cold water into a bath or basin first and then add the hot water to avoid her scalding herself. To use ordinary mixer faucets, teach her how to adjust these to a comfortable temperature.

A young child under six will probably not be able to reach the basin, so you should use a child step. As with the kitchen step, keep it in a low-level cabinet in the bathroom – perhaps in a built-in vanity unit below the basin, so that she can bring it out herself when needed and then put it away when she has finished with it.

So that your child can find her own towel, wash cloth, toothbrush and toothpaste easily, make sure you have a low-level towel rod, a low-level shelf for toothbrush and toothpaste and a low level mirror so that she can see herself, full-length. If there is a mirror on the wall, try to make sure it goes right down to the basin level so that she can really see herself cleaning her teeth.

Show her as early as possible how to use the doorknob and the lock. In this way there will be no danger of her locking herself in – it is the child who has been over-protected and never allowed to use a key, who experiments one day and finds herself locked in a room! In a Montessori classroom, children are introduced to different

types of locks and keys as early as two and a half or three, but if you are worried about this level of independence at that age, you can compromise by installing locks that can be opened from the outside in an emergency!

WATER PLAY

Water play is very important for young children, and they will always enjoy bath time. Perhaps a low-level cupboard under the sink could have a shelf in it for bath toys, or you could keep a basket for toys somewhere in the bathroom. Use a plastic string bag to store wet bath toys, and hang it from the faucet so that the toys drain into the bath rather than all over the floor.

Provide plenty of cups and pourers – children can spend valuable time playing pouring games in the bath, and this experience of understanding the properties of water cannot be overestimated. Using a mild bubble bath can be an excellent idea, too, and your child will enjoy experimenting with the bubbles. Point out to her how reflections are different in the curved surface of the bubbles, and how you can sometimes see the colors of the rainbow in them.

Practical life activities

Encourage your child to help with all the

From an early age, encourage your child to be independent and to care for herself through practical life activities, such as washing her hands, brushing her own teeth, and learning to keep the bathroom clean and neat.

cleaning jobs in the bathroom, such as the bath and the wash basin, polishing the faucets, using the toilet brush, cleaning the floor, folding the towels and wiping the surfaces. All of these activities will take a little longer if your child is helping, but she will thoroughly enjoy all of them and so will you.

THE HALL AND STAIRS

Many parents use gates either at the top or at the bottom of the stairs to prevent accidents. Montessori recommended that you try to do without them: instead, spend the time showing your child how to go up and down stairs safely by herself. Your baby may well try to climb the stairs while she is still crawling, so you are going to need to be vigilant if you are going to avoid tumbles, but it is worth persevering. It is surprising how quickly a baby or toddler will learn to go up, turn around and come back down again backward, and many babies develop a high degree of skill, whizzing up and down stairs quite safely by the age of twelve to fifteen months. Always be with them until they are older.

Walking down stairs properly is a longer term project, as your toddler will have to feel safe on her two legs to start with. Obviously she is not going to learn this skill in a short time; she will need plenty of practice, and you will have to have the time to spend with her while she does. It is worth bearing in mind, however, that it is usually the overprotected child who has not been allowed to develop the skill of climbing who is more likely to have an accident. If you wish to provide some support while still encouraging her independence, install a second banister, lower than the standard one, at child height. This can easily be removed as the child grows tall enough to hold the adult rail, but it will be there to help her while she is still little.

If coats and other outdoor gear are kept in the hall, make sure there is a set of child-height hooks for your child and her friends to hang their

(Left) Free to go up and down stairs to her bedroom whenever she wishes, this child has confidence, and a feeling of security in her own home.
(Right) On arriving home, this child goes straight to the hall closet, where there is a hook at the right height for her. The routine is quickly established and the child enjoys doing things for herself.

things. It's also a good idea to have a rack or box near the door, so that they learn always to remove their outdoor shoes or rubber boots and put on indoor shoes or slippers before going any farther into the house. If you have a utility room with an outside door to the back or side, you may prefer to put a box nearby to keep mud from accumulating in the hall.

Who comes in?
The hall is a good place to identify who comes to the house. Give your child a big notebook or scrapbook to note down in pictures and words (written by you if she is too young to write them in herself) everyone who comes to the door in a particular week. This might include regulars like the mailman, your child's babysitter if she has one, or her friends, her grandparents, your adult friends and relations, or occasional visitors like salesmen or women.

Practical life activities
These could include such activities as cleaning the stairs with an appropriately-sized brush and pan, polishing the banisters and dusting window sills and baseboards.

GAMES AND ACTIVITIES TO PLAY

THE VALUE OF GAMES

There are many reasons why it is a good idea to play games with your child, but perhaps the most important one is that it will involve your child's active participation with you, the parent, and help to build a sound and rewarding relationship between the two of you. Another good reason is that children enjoy games, and the ones chosen here are appropriate for their age and development, so they will attract and hold their attention. Games are also excellent for helping the child develop intellectually – she will learn a lot of new facts, and they encourage problem-solving and memory skills.

Games help social development as well because they usually involve taking turns, co-operating with others and handling different situations. Finally, they help develop physical skills like manual dexterity and coordination.

USING THE GAMES IN THIS BOOK

The games and activities in this book have been chosen because they can be played by you with your child, or by children in groups, pairs, or alone. Most can be played indoors or out, and have been described in the appropriate sections of this book so that they can be played in conjunction with the other learning experiences and activities suggested in them.

The games are grouped by age, although these are not rigid since development is a very individual process. You are the person best placed to decide whether your child is ready and capable of playing something indicated here as being suitable for older children.

Games and activities that have been suggested for the younger child are very simple and will build upon the knowledge that she is likely to have acquired. They will also help her to develop the basic skills necessary for playing games with others, for example, the idea of taking turns and making simple moves. As language skills develop, more complex ideas have been included.

Word games are excellent for a variety of occasions. For example, they not only can be played at home, but also in waiting rooms, on car journeys and elsewhere. Some games have been introduced here and the appropriate age levels indicated.

Computer games are becoming more and more popular, and there are a number that have been designed to give children practice in counting and spelling.

Finally, games can help parents to identify and solve problems that may have developed. A good tip for parents is to observe their child for a period of time and notice what keeps her happiest. Then try to provide her with this activity regularly and perhaps develop a game around it that involves the skills that you have noticed need developing.

For ease of use, and so that the purpose is clear right from the start, I have grouped the activities that follow under subject headings and they progress from the simplest to the more complex. Don't let this disguise the very important fact that all of them are, above all, fun to play. Try some and see – and enjoy!

STAGES OF PLAY AND CHOOSING AN APPROPRIATE GAME

Each child is an individual having a different personality, experiencing a different world around her that is unique to her. Even if two children of the same age live in the same neighborhood, they could have vastly different experiences. They may be the youngest of three, the oldest child, or a middle child. They may live

GAMES AND ACTIVITIES

in a one-parent family or an extended family. The mother may be at home all day or only for a few hours. Furthermore, these two children may be at different stages in their development, although they may have exactly the same chronological age. So it is important to understand that the games suggested for a particular age group are not arbitrary. Remember that the Montessori philosophy is: – *observe your child and meet her individual needs.*

LANGUAGE AND READING GAMES

THE SILENCE GAME
AGE 2 TO 6 YEARS

This is a game that can be played anywhere – indoors or out. Maria Montessori developed it when she was working with partially deaf children. She stood at the back of the class, softly called out the name of each child in turn, and when the child heard her name, she went very quietly to her. Since their hearing was impaired, they had to listen very hard, and their response was to be very quiet as well.

On another occasion she went to visit a class of normal children all under five. On the way there, she met a mother carrying a baby, took the baby and went into the classroom. When the children came up to look at the baby, she said, "Look, how still the baby lies. Can you be as quiet as he is?" To her surprise, the children became very quiet. She noticed how much they enjoyed this and played the silence game with them – using the same technique as she had used with the deaf children. Every time she played the game, she noticed how much the children enjoyed it and how rested they appeared after it. From that time on, the Silence Game has always been played in Montessori classrooms.

How it helps your child
The sheer enjoyment children derive from it makes this a worthwhile game to play at home. It is also good for your child's auditory awareness as it helps her to become more attuned to different sounds around her and to develop control. If played by several members of the family, it can create a sense of unity and togetherness. Montessori also believed that it helped develop a spiritual awareness.

How to play
Ask your child to sit down and see if she can be really quiet. Never impose silence upon her – it must be mutually agreed. Explain to her that to hear clearly it is easier if she keeps absolutely still. At first ask her what sounds she can hear. Depending on what room you are in, it may be the sound of cars, or planes going over outside, the sound of weather – wind or rain – or the sound of birds in the garden, or even the sound of a machine, such as the dishwasher or the washing machine.

Keep the silence for a minute or more; then in a whisper ask her what she has heard. Talk about the noise. Is it loud or soft? Is it nice to listen to, or is it too noisy? This is a game that can be played at any time of the day or in any place, with any number of participants. Children always enjoy it and learn from it.

THE OBJECT GAME
AGE 3 TO 4 YEARS

How it helps your child
This is a game that should be played around the time your child is learning letter sounds. It helps her to identify and analyze different sounds.

What you need
A group of small objects all beginning with the same letter – a box, a ball, a bead, a button, a book. A second group of objects beginning with another letter such as a puzzle, a pencil, a pin.

How to play
1. Lay out the first group of objects on a table.

2. Point to them one at a time, say the word and make sure your child can hear the "b" at the beginning of each word.

3. Then add a few more objects, but this time choose the second group, the ones beginning with the letter "p" and make sure she can hear the sound.

4. Pick up one of the things beginning with "b" and say: "I spy with my little eye something else beginning with b."

5. Ask your child to choose one of the other things that begin with "b," showing that she can hear the sound in a word. If she gets it wrong, a good way of handling the error is to pronounce the word with the incorrect sound, i.e., "Is this a b-bencil?" This would give the child the opportunity to correct her own error rather than being told she is wrong. Gently explain which is the right one, and then play the game again.

VARIATION 1
Place only two things on the table, say a book and a pencil. Then say: "I am going to pick up the thing that begins with 'b'. Which is it?" Your child should point to the object and say the word.

VARIATION 2
Choose objects that are three letter "phonic" words, such box, cup, hat, etc. Say the words, emphasizing each individual letter b-o-x, c-u-p, and so on. Then play another version of "I spy" by saying: "I spy something with a 'p' sound at the end of it." Your child should pick up the cup.

INSETS FOR DESIGN
AGE 4 TO 5 YEARS

How it helps your child
It gives her indirect preparation for writing because your child learns how to use and control

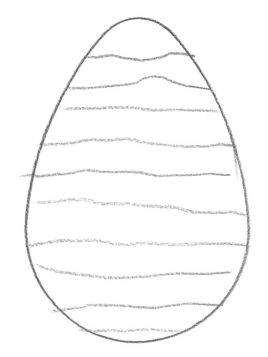

a pencil, making straight lines and curves similar to the strokes that will be used when she begins to write letters.

What you need
Geometric shapes (square, sphere, etc.).
Colored pencils
Small squares of paper
Make your own shapes by cutting the recommended ones from cardboard.

How to play
1. Ask your child to choose one shape, such as a triangle.

2. Show her how to place it carefully over a square piece of paper and draw around the inside of the triangle, using one of the colored pencils.

3. Remove the geometric shape, and she will have drawn a triangle. Show her how to fill in the space in the middle of the triangle using a different color pencil. The lines should be

controlled, straight lines (see illustration), not scribbles. She can eventually choose different shapes and put them together to make patterns and designs. It is important to know that this is not a coloring exercise; it is controlled drawing which helps develop control of the pencil.

SANDPAPER LETTERS
AGE 4 TO 5 YEARS

How it helps your child
This activity should be done simultaneously with the Insets for Design activity above and, like it, gives indirect preparation for writing because the child is feeling the shapes of the letters she will eventually write. It is also indirect preparation for reading because you teach her the phonic sounds of the letters. When she knows them, she will be able to sound out simple phonic words, such as cat and dog.

What you need
A set of letters of the alphabet made from sandpaper
These letters can be obtained commercially. You can also make them yourself by cutting them out from sandpaper and mounting them on cardboard. Use small letters.

How to play
To teach the letter sounds, you will find it easy if you use the same approach as Montessori teachers. The lesson is in three stages and is called the "Three Period Lesson."

Choose two letters that are different in shape and sound, such as "c" and "m."

1. **The first stage.** Place one of the letters in front of your child and tell her: "This is 'c'." Ask her to trace the letter with her index finger and, while she is doing this, repeat again the sound "c."

Take away the letter "c" and put the other letter shape in front her, and say: "This is 'm'." Repeat the procedure.

2. **The second stage.** Next, put both letters in front of her and ask her: "Please show me which one is 'c'?"; and then: "Which one is 'm'?"

3. **The third stage.** If she gets it right, then point to the "m" and say to her "What is this?" Then ask the same question pointing to the "c." The child should be able to tell you.

Follow this up by mentioning some words beginning with "m" such as "mom" and some beginning with "c" such as "cat." Over a period of days, teach your child more letters.

Always try to make this game a happy experience; never try to force your child to participate. If you have taught her when she is ready, she will learn them all very quickly – in just a matter of a few weeks.

MOVABLE ALPHABET
AGE 4 TO 5 YEARS

How it helps your child
This game will help her practice listening for the sounds in words, and it is preparation for reading. The idea is to build a word starting with the sounds and then, by putting the sounds together quickly, saying the word. Your child will suddenly realize she can read by sounding out the letters.

What you need
Five sets of individual letters of the alphabet
A box of small objects, such as a toy cat, dog, etc.
Cut out the letters from cardboard and collect the objects from a child's dolls' house. Other objects could be a pen, a box, a cup – anything small that is a three-letter phonic word.

How to play

1. Ask your child to choose one of the objects. She may choose the cat. Ask her what sounds she can hear in "cat." She will probably say "c" so ask her to find it among the letters.

2. Then ask what sound comes next in the word "cat." When she says "a" ask her to find it.

3. Finally, ask her if there are any other sounds in "cat" and hopefully she will say "t." So you ask her to find the "t." You then build the word and read it to her.

After lots of practice with lots of different three letter words, one day she will recognize the word she has built – she is reading!

The next stage in the reading process is to give her more practice in reading phonic words. In a Montessori school, this is done by a series of exercises using pictures and cards. A commercially produced reading program is available for those who wish to follow up at home. Even if you do not continue with this graded approach to reading, keep on enjoying reading stories with her and allowing her to read the words she recognizes occasionally. Within a short space of time, she will be reading more and more words and will, from the sense, also be able to read words that are not phonic.

WORDS AROUND THE HOUSE
AGE 5 TO 6 YEARS

How it helps your child
This game helps to extend vocabulary.

What you need
A set of small white cards with one word on each card. The words should be objects around the house, such as table, chair, door, and so on. You can make a set of cards for each room.

How to play

1. Read the words with your child.

2. Ask her to go and place the cards by the objects they describe.

3. You can vary the game and make it more fun by placing the cards face down so that she cannot see them. You then look at one and describe the object, asking her to guess what is written on the card.

4. Another variation is to ask her to place the cards on the "Plan of the House" described on page 72. This is a game she can play by herself.

SENSORY DEVELOPMENT GAMES

MYSTERY BAG GAME
AGE 2 TO 3 YEARS

How it helps your child
This game gives your child practice in identifying and naming objects only through the sense of touch.

What you need
2 identical bags, each with a cord to close the top
2 sets of small geometric objects, such as a cube, a sphere, a cone, a cylinder, a pyramid and a prism
One set of objects should be put into each bag.

How to play

1. Get your child to hold one bag and you hold the other.

2. Put your hand inside your bag and select one of the objects, say the cube, bring it out and show it to her.

3. Ask her to put her hands inside her bag and try to find the same shape, using only her sense of touch. She is not allowed to look inside the bag.

4. Continue the game in this way until all the objects have been taken out of your bag.

VARIATION

Although this Montessori game is specifically designed to help children learn geometric shapes, you could play a simple version with younger children using small objects with different shapes and textures, like wooden beads, a ring, a crayon, a spool, a small table tennis or golf ball, a piece of Lego, a toy car, etc. See if your child can identify them in the same way.

"SORTING BY SOUND" BINGO

AGE 3 TO 4 YEARS

How it helps your child
This game develops listening and memory skills. It can be played by a parent and child, or by a group of children.

What you need
2 or more bingo cards with six different pictures on each, illustrating things that make a different sound. (Say, a pig, a cow, an airplane, a vacuum cleaner, a bird, a car.) You can make them by pasting pictures from magazines on thin cardboard which you have marked in squares.
A set of separate cards, showing each of the objects contained on the bingo cards.

How to play
For 2 to 6 players
1. Keep one bingo card and give your child or children the others. Place the set of individual cards face down on a table.

2. Begin the game by picking up a card, turning it over and making the noise of the thing depicted by the picture.

3. Ask your child to guess what it is. If she is right and she has it on her bingo card, she

takes the picture and places it on the bingo card, on the matching square.

4. She then picks a card from the individual pile and make the appropriate sound for you to name in your turn. If you don't have it on your card, return the card to the bottom of the pile. The winner is the one to fill up her bingo card first.

SENSO

AGE 4 TO 5 YEARS

How it helps your child
This game encourages perceptual development by giving your child sensory experiences of texture and shape.

What you need
4 game boards, each with nine different shapes and textures pasted onto them. Each board should be color-coded.
36 separate individual cards, one for each of the

shapes mounted on the game boards, color-coded to the appropriate board.

This game can be obtained commercially. To make it at home, cut out two copies of each of the appropriate shapes (see illustration) from sandpaper. Mount one set of nine shapes on each of four large squares of cardboard to make game boards. Mount the second set of shapes on individual cards.

How to play

For 4 players

1. Each player chooses a board, and the corresponding squares for the board are placed in front of her.

2. Each player is asked to feel the shape on a square and then to find the corresponding shape on her game board. So that the child does not select by sight, place the game board upside down and ask her to lift it up and feel the shape underneath.

VARIATION

Ask the players to find a particular shape, size or number of the shapes on their boards – for instance, three circles, or a large square.

MEMOS

AGE 5 TO 6 YEARS

How it helps your child

This game helps develop perceptual as well as motor and memory skills.

What you need

1 game board with 48 holes covered by disks. The board should be hollow in the middle so that a "command" card can be slotted into it (see photograph).

(Above) Slot the command card into the board and (Below) Play the game!

8 "command" cards, each containing two sets of different items – geometric shapes, toys, color combinations, musical instruments, patterns, motor vehicles, numbers, animals, etc. The cards should have an increasing level of difficulty – some could be suitable for a younger child and some for six year olds and above.

How to play
For 2 or more players
1. Select a command card and insert it into the slot.

2. Each player takes a turn and lifts off two disks revealing pictures underneath.

3. If the two pictures do not match, then the disks are replaced, and the players try to remember the location of the pictures.

4. If the pictures make a pair, the player can remove the disks and keep them.
   The object of the game is to match the pictures and thereby collect the most number of disks.

MATHEMATICS GAMES

SORTING BUTTONS
AGE 2 TO 3 YEARS

How it helps your child
This game gives her experience in sorting into sets, a good preparation for mathematics.

What you need
Place 3 or 4 dishes or saucers on a tray, with a larger dish for the middle.
Provide 3 or 4 sets of matching buttons, each set different in size and color. (Place all of the sets of buttons in the larger dish.)

How to play
1. Your child can play this game by herself. Ask her to close her eyes or put on a blindfold.

(Some children find blindfolds disturbing, so if you suggest this, make sure that you use something soft like a scarf, and don't tie it too tightly.)

2. Show your child how to feel the buttons and sort them by size into different dishes until they have all been used up.

3. Get her to take off the blindfold or open her eyes – the color of the buttons will indicate whether or not she has sorted them correctly.

FLAT SHAPES
AGE 3 TO 4 YEARS

How it helps your child
This game gives your child experience in sorting different geometric shapes by touch and by sight. It prepares her for geometry later.

What you need
3 sets of geometric shapes, one with straight sides (square, rectangle, triangle), one with curved (circle, oval), and one with a mixture of straight and curved (semicircle, etc.). Each set should be white on one side and a different color on the other – say green for one set, orange for the second and black for the third.
3 sets of cards illustrating all the shapes described above, one outlined in solid color, the second with thick lines and the third with thin lines.

How to play
1. Take the sets of geometric shapes and lay them all out, white side up.

2. Ask your child to feel around them and sort them into the three sets.

3. When she has done this, she turns over the cards, and if the colors are the same in each set, green, orange and black, then the geometric shapes have been sorted correctly.

VARIATION

Take the first set of cards with the geometric shapes marked out, and sort them according to the attributes – straight sides, curved sides and straight and curved sides. To check if the cards are sorted correctly, your child matches the geometric shapes and the colors against the drawn shapes on the cards. This same game can then be repeated with the second and then the third set of cards.

Here a child is matching different shapes to individual cards depicting the shape in outline. An easy game to make, and hours of concentration and enjoyment for the child.

PICKIN

AGE 4 TO 5 YEARS

How it helps your child
This game gives your child practice in simple addition and subtraction.

What you need
1 game board that has two rows of eleven circles into which the disks, below, can fit
11 disks numbered from 0 to 10
A 12-sided dice
This game can be obtained commercially. To make it at home, create a large game board from

cardboard (see photograph). Use plastic disks, or cut out small disks from cardboard; then write the appropriate number on each one.

Pickin is a great game for children of all ages – a good one for older sister to play with younger brother, and it will help both to improve their number skills.

How to play
For 2 players
1. Place the disks in order from 0 to 10 on one side of the game board.

2. Throw the dice to see who goes first; the highest number wins. The first player throws the dice again and choses two disks from her opponent's side which add up to the number she has thrown.

3. She places these disks on her side of the game board and throws again.

4. She continues to throw a number and take from her opponent until she can no longer make up the number she has thrown.

5. The dice then passes to the other player, who throws the dice and tries to take back all the disks in the same way. The game continues in this way until all the disks are on one side of the game board.

VARIATION
Use the idea of subtraction, rather than addition.

66

CUBICO
AGE 5 TO 6 YEARS

How it helps your child
This game gives your child experience in addition and subtraction.

What you need
1 large board, divided into nine squares
9 six-sided cubes with numbers on all six sides; the six sides should be colored red, green, orange, brown, blue and purple. Each cube should contain the following numbers:

	Red	Green	Orange	Brown	Blue	Purple
Cube 1	1	33	21	13	5	14
Cube 2	18	14	12	27	3	2
Cube 3	28	19	7	4	2	13
Cube 4	17	9	24	16	13	12
Cube 5	24	16	19	11	8	5
Cube 6	52	5	22	7	10	18
Cube 7	23	25	9	6	4	15
Cube 8	34	8	15	14	6	17
Cube 9	11	3	43	10	1	32

This game can be obtained commercially. To make it at home, make a large board from cardboard or heavy paper, then mark it off into equal-sized squares large enough to contain one of the cubes. Make the cubes from paper, color each side in a different color as above, then number as above. The color coding acts as a "control of error."

How to play
1. Ask your child to turn the cubes over until each cube has the same color facing upward.

2. Ask her to place the cubes in a square so that the sum of the first two vertically and horizontally equals the number on the third cube (see diagram in the next column for the correct sequences).

Red Series			Green Series		
17	11	28	3	16	19
1	23	24	5	9	14
18	34	52	8	25	33

Orange Series			Brown Series		
7	15	22	10	4	14
12	9	21	6	7	13
19	24	43	16	11	27

Blue Series			Purple Series		
1	4	5	2	12	14
2	6	8	13	5	18
3	10	13	15	17	32

SCIENCE AND NATURE GAMES AND ACTIVITIES

COOKING
AGE 2 TO 3 YEARS

How it helps your child
When baking or preparing food, involve your child in the activity as much as possible – there are many recipe books written specially for young children. If they help you with your cooking, they will be learning scientific concepts as well as being useful and having fun – for example, the way different things dissolve in water, how substances change with heat and cold, etc.

What you need
A few cooking utensils appropriate in size for a small pair of hands to use, and lots of time and patience.

How to play

At first give your child simple tasks, such as mixing flour and water. Remember to demonstrate things slowly and always use new words – stir, whisk, beat, etc. Later, she could progress to making something of her own like cookies or gingerbread.

FLOATING AND SINKING GAME

AGE 3 TO 4 YEARS

How it helps your child

Play this after your child has experienced the concepts of floating and sinking using actual objects, something which you can do with her in the bath or at the kitchen sink. You could see which fruit and which vegetables float and sink, for instance. It will help her to remember which objects float and which sink.

What you need

A large picture of a bowl containing water and a set of pictures of objects to be used in the experiment.

How to play

1. Ask your child to select the pictures one by one, and place them either over the top of the water in the bowl, or on the bottom of the bowl, depending upon what she has discovered about floating and sinking.

2. If she gets any wrong, show her with real objects and water whether the object floats or sinks and then play the game with the pictures the next day.

BODY PARTS

AGE 4 TO 5 YEARS

How it helps your child

It will make her more aware of the parts of her body and how they work. This will help her to think about how her own body functions.

The starting point of this activity is fun, with mother drawing around her child to make an outline of her body. When this is finished, they discover together where the joints should be and then begin to cut up the parts before putting them back together again.

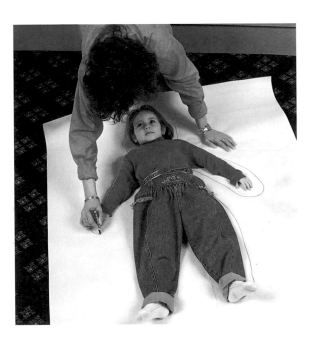

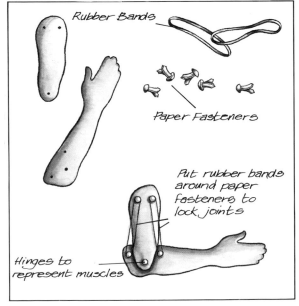

Rubber Bands

Paper Fasteners

Put rubber bands around paper fasteners to lock joints

Hinges to represent muscles

What you need

A large piece of white cardboard – this should be larger than your child (see photograph)
Some fasteners and a marker pen

How to play

1. Talk to her about the human body and all the different parts, then ask her which parts she can move and which parts she can't. Explain what a joint is and ask her to find all the joints in her hands, arms, legs, feet, and so on.

2. Draw an outline of her body and together mark where the joints are located on it.

3. Cut out the drawing at the joints and then put the pieces together again with fasteners and rubber bands (see diagrams).

4. When this is done, talk about her backbone and link it to the animal classification game (see page 111). She has discovered that she, too, is a vertebrate animal.

FOOD GROUPS GAME
AGE 5 TO 6 YEARS

How it helps your child

This activity will teach her about the basic food groups we need and develop an awareness in her of healthy eating.

What you need

A large sheet of paper
Pictures of different food. You can cut these out of magazines, draw them yourself or ask your child to draw them.
Double-sided tape

How to play

1. Divide the piece of paper into seven sections and head each one with a different food group: fruit and vegetables, meat, milk and milk products, bread, cereals, oils, and sugar.

2. Every time you have a meal, discuss what you have eaten, choose a suitable picture and stick it on your chart. At the end of a day, you can discuss together what you have eaten and decide what you may need more of on another day.

HISTORY GAMES AND ACTIVITIES

STORIES AND RHYMES ABOUT TIME
AGE 2 TO 3 YEARS

How it helps your child

Stories and rhymes are a way of attracting and holding attention. Children can get very involved and learn many new ideas and words.

What you need

A selection of stories and rhymes about time and stories relating to things that happened a long time ago.
Some suggestions are: *Hickory, Dickory Dock, the Mouse Ran Up The Clock*, etc. (A children's rhyme book will give you the complete rhyme and other suggestions.)

How to play

You can "play" (by reading the stories to her) at any time. Try to include finger play and other activities, both to involve her in the stories and to highlight the ideas they contain.

TIMELINE OF YOUR CHILD'S DAY
AGE 3 TO 4 YEARS

How it helps your child

She will develop a sense of time with this game. It is particularly good because it depicts the experiences your child will herself remember, and it gives her a pictorial view of time.

What you need

A long sheet of paper, about 18 inches wide, divided into sections marked off in hours, starting say with 7:00 a.m. and ending whenever she goes to bed. Include a clock face, too.
Pencils and crayons
Paste or tape

How to play

1. Ask your child to draw a picture of herself when she gets up in the morning, for example, getting out of bed or having breakfast. Discuss with her what she is going to do next, and eventually you will get her to remember that after breakfast she goes to school, plays in the backyard, has lunch, walks home, goes shopping, has supper, watches television, reads stories, has a bath, and goes to bed. As and when she feels like it, she can draw another picture.

2. Paste or tape these pictures to the timeline at the appropriate time of the day.

3. Pin it up in her bedroom or somewhere else where she can often look at it and reflect on her daily activities.

TIMELINE OF YOUR CHILD'S LIFE

AGE 4 TO 5 YEARS

How it helps your child

This variation on the basic timeline will help an older child develop a seqential perspective about the events of her life — often at this age, everything that has already passed happened

Creating her own timeline can be great fun for a child – and it can be as long or as short as she wishes. This child had a very full morning, so will complete the rest of her timeline later!

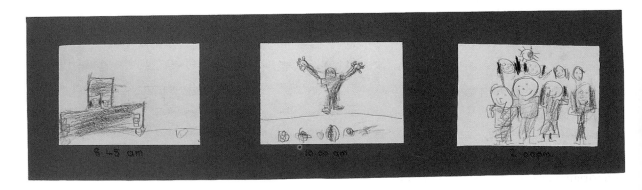

"yesterday" and everything that is going to happen will be "tomorrow." Time is one of the most difficult concepts for her to understand. The more experiences and discussions you have the better.

What you need
A large strip of paper divided into six sections (although it is suggested you do this with four or five year olds, you will eventually continue the activity with your child – hence the six sections); each section represents one year of your child's life.
A selection of photographs of your child at different times since birth
Paste or pins

How to play
1. Pin or paste the pictures on the timeline in the appropriate year. Talk to her about herself when she was a baby and let her ask questions.

2. Choose pictures that clearly show how much she has changed over the years.

TIMELINE OF HOMES THROUGH THE AGES
AGE 5 TO 6 YEARS

How it helps your child
It encourages her to think about changes that have occurred over a very long period of time and what influences have brought them about, and helps her to understand sequences of events.

What you need
A long strip of paper – wallpaper cut in half lengthwise is suitable. Divide the paper into at least six or seven sections, and mark these sections into centuries and years.
Examples of appropriate historical homes, such as Caves, Roman Villa, Middle Ages, Tudor, Victorian, early 1900s and a modern home

(You can sometimes find appropriate pictures in museums, or you can draw pictures copying them from books.)
Paste or tape

How to play
1. Start by talking about your own home and the things that are important. For example, we all sleep in beds, we prepare food each day and cook it, and we keep ourselves clean.

2. Show your child the pictures you have collected, and ask her if she can notice anything different about how the cooking was done long ago by the cavemen. The important thing is to encourage her to notice the similarities and differences herself.

3. Now go on to discuss why they did things differently, and perhaps look up some of the important inventions that have made modern life so comfortable and easy. For example, life has changed radically with the invention of electricity – electric bulbs were first used in 1879, refrigerators in 1879, the electric iron in 1882, the first electric oven in 1889, the electric toaster in 1909, the electric kettle as recently as 1923, and the electric dishwasher in 1899.

This game could be linked with an appropriate museum visit, which would make all these historical events very graphic for young children.

GEOGRAPHY GAMES

OLD MOTHER HUBBARD
AGE 2 TO 3 YEARS

How it helps your child
She will love this game because it is silly, but it will also focus her attention on where things are kept in the house and she will begin to develop spatial awareness.

These pictures, cut from a Sunday newspaper magazine, depict most of the significant furniture found in a house. These pictures are then pasted on to a house plan, helping the child learn about the different functions of rooms and furniture.

What you need
Lots of time!

How to play
1. First teach your child the traditional kindergarden rhyme below.

OLD MOTHER HUBBARD

Old Mother Hubbard
Went to the cupboard,
To fetch her poor dog a bone;
But when she got there
The cupboard was bare
And so the poor dog had none

2. Then vary it by saying: "Old Mother Hubbard went to the cupboard to look for some sheets, which cupboard was that?" Go through a list of many things that are found in the linen cupboard, the bathroom cabinet, the closet, and ask what else she will find there. Eventually you will get to the kitchen cupboard and you say, "It was bare!"

PLAN OF THE HOUSE
AGE 3 TO 4 YEARS

How it helps your child
This is a simple way of getting your child to think about the various places in the house and how they can be represented on a kind of map.

What you need
A large piece of paper
Pictures cut from magazines of different furniture

in the house, such as a bed, a kitchen table, a refrigerator, a chair, a stove, etc.
Crayons or pencils
Paste or tape

How to play

1. Draw a house, put in the roof and perhaps a garage. Divide the house into rooms, as in your home.

2. Discuss with your child what all the rooms in the house are and what we are likely to find in them.

3. Ask her to select the appropriate furniture pictures for each room and stick them to the drawing in the right room.

WHERE DO I LIVE?

AGE 4 TO 5 YEARS

How it helps your child

It helps her to develop an awareness of how other people live.

What you need

A collection of pictures of different types of houses such as an igloo, a houseboat, a cottage, a mud hut, an apartment building, etc.
A similar collection of animal homes – for instance a bird's nest, a squirrel's drey, etc. and pictures of the animals, too
All pictures should be mounted on cardboard

How to play

1. Talk about the different types of houses. Describe what they are made of, where they are to be found, how old they might be, what they are called. See how many different types of houses there are.

2. Then show your child the photographs of human houses and ask her to identify the who lives where.

3. This could lead on to homes that animals live in.

4. Then you can play snap with the cards, matching the animals to their homes.
(There is a Turn Over Game with animal homes later in the book (see page 112.)

EXPERIMENTS WITH WATER IN THE KITCHEN

AGE 5 TO 6 YEARS

How it helps your child

Your child will be able to witness the effects of temperature and actually see that water can be a solid, liquid, or gas. "Kitchen sink" experiments encourage observation and questioning, which are skills needed for later learning in school. These activities will also help her to understand how the water cycle works and how this affects the changes that occur in the weather – leading to an understanding of geography.

What you need

8 empty herb jars to make Montessori thermic bottles. Fill two jars with cold water, two with warm water, two with fairly hot water and two with hot water (not hot enough to burn).
A kettle and an ice cube tray for the second stage of the experiment (see overleaf).

How to play

1. The first stage is to develop an awareness of temperature. Ask your child to close her eyes and feel the jars, then pair them so that there are two cold, two warm, two fairly hot and two hot jars.

2. Explain to her how you create the different water temperatures. If you have a kitchen thermometer, take the temperature of the

water and try to discover the boiling point and freezing point of water.

3. Show her how, by boiling a kettle, when water reaches "boiling point" it turns to steam which escapes as a gas – and make sure she realizes that it rises, never falls.

4. Put some water into an ice tray in the freezer and leave it to freeze. Show her how the water has turned to ice and become solid, and discuss the temperature, the "freezing point," at which this took place.

5. Explain about the water cycle: how every day the sun heats up the sea and the water in rivers and lakes, and some of the water turns to vapor (gas); how this vapor rises, like the steam from the kettle, that as it rises it cools and forms tiny water droplets, which make clouds; how eventually the droplets collide with each other, grow in size and come back to earth as rain; that rain sometimes, when it is cold enough, falls as snow or hail. Back on earth the water cycle begins again. (Many books show pictures of the water cycle.)

ARTS AND CRAFT ACTIVITIES

PRINTING HANDS AND FEET
AGE 2 TO 3 YEARS

How it helps your child
This activity develops her sense of design and imagination.

What you need
Poster paints
A brush
A blank sheet of paper

How to play
1. Help your child to put the paint straight on her hands using a paint brush, first one hand and then the other.

2. Tell her to press her hand firmly on the paper. Eventually, you can encourage her to make patterns.

3. Repeat the activity with her feet, making sure the paper is large enough.

TEARING AND CUTTING
AGE 3 TO 4 YEARS

How it helps your child
It develops her awareness of shapes and sizes, helps increase her control of the finger muscles and provides an opportunity to express her ideas.

What you need
Tissue paper
Old magazines and newspapers
Glue
Some thicker paper for mounting the pictures

How to play
1. Show your child how to hold the magazines or newspapers with two hands, then how to pull and tear with the dominant hand. Allow her to tear the paper into any shape and for as long as she wishes.

2. When she has mastered this skill, show her how to tear strips and squares.

3. After a considerable pile of paper has been prepared, suggest she draws an outline of, say,

Making a recognizable print on paper using her hand, is an absorbing activity for this young child. The position of the hand can be varied to make different patterns.

a house or tree and then show her how to glue on the torn paper. With practice the pictures can become more complex in design and shape.

Never impose an idea on your child. It is important that she has the freedom to explore the materials and make her own creations.

COLLAGE
AGE 4 TO 5 YEARS

How it helps your child
The tactile nature of collage makes it an activity that your child can enjoy doing with her hands. It can be very creative because the variety of materials that can be used will produce different effects.

What you need
Background material such as cardboard, thick paper, wood, corkboard, paper plates or a large piece of fabric
A collection of assorted materials such as tissue paper, decorative or wrapping papers, cloth, wool, string; in fact, almost any waste materials
Something with which to attach the materials to the background, such as glue, tape, staples.

How to play
1. To begin with, just allow your child to get used to gluing.

2. Then suggest she draws an outline of something such as a bird or a larger picture of, say, a garden scene, or even a geometric pattern.

3. Suggest that she fills in the entire outline by gluing on the various materials.

SEWING
AGE 5 TO 6 YEARS

Children can start sewing at a much earlier age than five. The preparatory stages for a three year old are threading large beads, leading on to thick sewing cards with the holes readymade. By the age of five you can introduce your child to sewing using Sida – a special type of material with large holes.

How it helps your child
These activities develop fine motor skills, encourage concentration and can be very satisfying.

What you need
A selection of large needles – not too blunt as it will be too difficult to sew, and she will give up. (A Montessori parent is not afraid to use a needle with a sharp end!)
A selection of cotton and silk threads
Some firm materials, such as felt or linen

How to play
1. First show your child how to do a simple running stitch and later introduce more complex ones, such as cross stitch, chain stitch and buttonhole stitch.

2. Always make something that has a purpose and that your child can see that you use in the home.

Appliqué and patchwork are other simple sewing techniques that interested six year olds could easily master.

Here, a five-year-old boy is making a first attempt at "real" sewing. The embroidered Sida can be used as a table mat when it is finished.

Exploring the Neighborhood

INTRODUCTION

As you have already seen, your child absorbs knowledge from his surroundings from a very young age, and this applies as much to the world outside your home as it does to his life within it – every time he leaves the house there is something new to experience. Some of these experiences will be initiated spontaneously by your child during the course of normal activities – he may kick a ball around in the garden, walk through a park picking up leaves, dig in a sand box, push a wheeled toy in the backyard, or walk along the street stopping from time to time to investigate things. There appears to be no particular point to the activity, but he is learning from the environment just the same.

Other experiences may be initiated by you with the intention of involving him in a learning situation. You may suggest your child helps you plant some flowers, for instance, or weeds the vegetable patch, or even helps to find the food in the supermarket.

Yet others could be initiated by him, but with participation by you as you spot an opportunity to point out something new – for instance, if he kicks over a stone in the garden, suggest that he looks under it to see if there are any creepie-crawlies.

Your role in all of this is to make sure that his home environment is stimulating and varied enough to provide all three types of experience, and that when he is alone he is one hundred percent safe.

THE NATURAL ENVIRONMENT

Montessori emphasized the importance of helping young children to understand the natural world, and she believed that learning about how things happen and work occurs in five progressive stages:

Stage One: Observation and discovery

A two year old will squat down and look at the smallest insects, pull apart the petals of flowers, and show an intense interest in discovering what happens to animals and plants and how they react to touch and other sensations. During this period, it is important to stimulate his interest in everyday things in the natural world. You could talk to him, for instance, about the seasons and tell him what to look for in each one. You will find that he gathers information at a tremendous rate and learns a lot more than you might think possible.

Stage Two: Care and responsibility

This is when he realizes that plants and animals in a domestic situation depend for their survival on

Enjoying the family cat brings happiness to this young girl. As well as this, she learns about his feeding requirements and way of life.

the care of humans. He will want to participate in this caring, and this is the time to teach him skills and give him specific responsibilities, such as feeding the cat every day or watering the potted plants. (Montessori was particularly keen on the value of cats and recommended that every household should have one.)

Stage Three: Processes and predictions

This is when he begins to understand the processes and the sequences involved in the natural world, and he learns how to predict with confidence and have expectations – he knows by now, for instance, that if he waits patiently, in the normal course of events bulbs will arrive in the spring and the suddenly plump cat will have her kittens and become thin again. During this time, encourage him to examine new information carefully and show him how to assess it and make new predictions.

Stage Four: Interdependence

At this point your child will show that he has not only developed a lot of knowledge about the animals and plants around him, but has grown to love and respect them, too. This is when you can explain the interdependence of living things, and such ideas as the food chain and how life depends on water and the gases in the air.

Stage Five: Cultivation and control

During this final stage he realizes that he has the power to cultivate and control the environment, changing it to meet his own needs and those of the community in which he lives. It is now that you can help him to understand the importance of saving habitats and species, and point out how easily the environment can be destroyed.

In each of the above stages, Montessori believed it was supremely important for adults to nurture a caring attitude to the environment so that the next generation would grow up in harmony with the natural world. Today this concept, of being *environmentally friendly*, has become even more desirable , and the best time to develop it in your child is when he is young. Perhaps, as a family, you could join an organization such as **Campaign to Care for the Earth** organized by the World Wide Fund for Nature or **Friends of the Earth** – both of these (and others like them) would not only help your child develop an awareness of the efforts being made worldwide to protect the planet, but also help him to understand what he could do as an individual to improve his own immediate environment.

Montessori felt that activities designed to help nurture an awareness of the natural environment were worthy in themselves, but she also stressed her belief that the child's spiritual development would benefit from this involvement as well. In an increasingly materialistic world, this aspect of development is often forgotten. Also, by being close to nature and becoming aware of the interdependence of all living things, your child will gradually develop an understanding of the universe as a whole.

THE MAN-MADE ENVIRONMENT

Even if you live in rural surroundings there will be a wealth of things that are man-made in your immediate neighborhood, and these, too, can provide valuable learning experiences for your child.

Developing an awareness of the different types of houses, roads and transportation in a town or village is just a beginning; other examples of man's ingenuity and exploitation of his habitat can be interesting as well – for instance, how he makes use of minerals and how he discovered electricity. Of course, environments are social and cultural, too, and looking at customs and traditions can also be fascinating.

An urban environment is just as enriching as a country or a suburban one, especially if you, as a parent, can take advantage of the many activities and places of interest that you can visit in your neighborhood.

IN THE BACKYARD

Your yard, however large or small, will provide a wealth of experiences for your child. From the first time he was taken into it as a very young baby, he would have received experiences through his senses, such as the feel of wind on his face or the sound of a bird singing, and by the time he is two, he will already have absorbed a lot.

To encourage a love of nature, you need only to spend time there together – just sit and watch and listen, or walk quietly around and touch and smell and, where appropriate, taste. Birds will come and go, and perhaps a squirrel will scurry across the trees, or a bee or butterfly will visit the flowers. Encourage your child to smell the flowers and touch the different leaves to discover their varied textures. Lie on the grass with him and watch the clouds moving across the sky and the patterns of the trees silhouetted against it. Play the Montessori Silence Game (see page 58) and talk about all the different sounds you both hear. Go out after dark sometimes and draw his attention to the many different sights and sounds of the night – the moon, the stars and the darkened sky.

THINGS WE FIND IN THE BACKYARD

You will find different types of soil and rocks in most yards. There is water in the soil or in ponds or puddles and usually a variety of plant and animal life, so your child can learn all about how plants and animals breathe, take in water, give out gases and reproduce. He could make a collection of different seeds and leaves, then sort and identify them, comparing their shape and size, and learn about the different uses of trees and plants.

Observing nature seems to come naturally to a young child – it is only necessary for you to create opportunities for him.

Creating an area in the yard for your child (Age 3 up)

A *vegetable patch* is a favorite with a young child. He can watch something grow from a seed to a vegetable, that he can prepare, cook and eat

SAFETY FIRST

First and foremost take special care when planning your yard to make it a safe place for your child to play in and explore by himself.

- Check access to and from the yard; gates should be self-latching and kept locked if they lead straight onto a dangerous road.

- Any sharp or power-driven gardening tools, such as a lawn mover, require expert handling and should be kept safely in a shed, a cupboard or a garage; so should fertilizers and garden sprays.

- There should be no access to the roof from the yard and open drains should be covered.

- Make a safe outdoor play area for, say, sand and water play for a very young child in full view of the kitchen or living room. Other suitable toys such as a swing, a seesaw or a jungle gym, should also be in full view, and you should teach your child how to use them safely.

- Take precautions if you have a swimming pool or pond. Agree some family rules and make sure your child understands them. Teach him how to swim as early as possible – two is not too soon.

- Make sure there are no poisonous plants such as poison oak or ivy, deadly nightshade, foxglove, lobelia, lily of the valley, wisteria, and toadstools in your yard.

himself. Choose a suitable part of the yard together, where there is enough sun and protection from wind.

First show him how to prepare the soil. Try to find garden tools that can easily be managed by small hands. Encourage him to feel the earth, its texture and its moistness. Explain that it doesn't matter if his hands get dirty as they can be washed after he has finished. Then choose one or more suitable vegetables that can be grown from seed – say, beans, broccoli, Brussels sprouts, cabbage, carrots, cauliflowers, leeks, onions, spinach, and many others. Show him how to plant them. Carefully read together the instructions on the pack of seeds so that they are planted under the right conditions, with enough space between them and at the right time of the year. Encourage

him to tend his garden regularly to enable the vegetables to grow.

If you have a large enough yard, suggest that he makes a herb garden in the same way.

While the seeds are growing outdoors, help him set up a seed-growing experiment in the house, planting either grass seeds on damp cotton wool or bean seeds in a jar with blotting paper and stones. He can then watch the roots grow down and the shoots strike up. An older child (five up) can measure how much growth there is each day and record it on graph paper.

As his plants are growing, make drawings, or cut out photographs, of the various parts of a plant (stem, petals, roots, leaves, stamen, etc.) and explain their function to him. Then make a game out of recognizing them (see page 111).

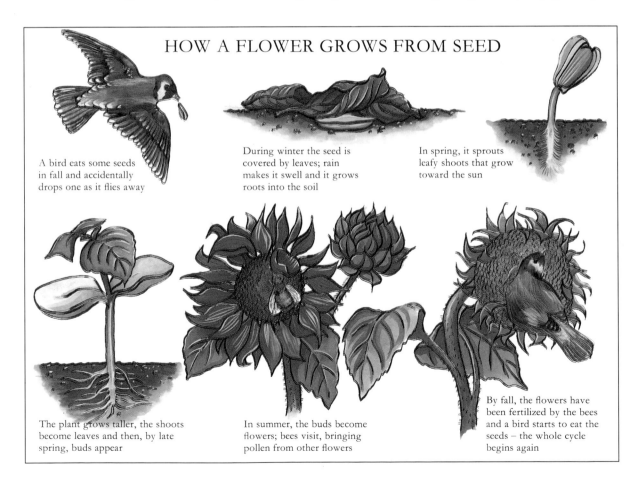

HOW A FLOWER GROWS FROM SEED

A bird eats some seeds in fall and accidentally drops one as it flies away

During winter the seed is covered by leaves; rain makes it swell and it grows roots into the soil

In spring, it sprouts leafy shoots that grow toward the sun

The plant grows taller, the shoots become leaves and then, by late spring, buds appear

In summer, the buds become flowers; bees visit, bringing pollen from other flowers

By fall, the flowers have been fertilized by the bees and a bird starts to eat the seeds – the whole cycle begins again

Attracting and keeping birds A table to feed birds could be another point of interest for a young child. Either buy one from a nursery or make one at home – all you need is a wooden pole and a square piece of wood. (see diagram). Hang a nut bag and a coconut shell or two on it, and regularly put out a variety of food such as bread, fruit, seeds and nuts. Encourage your child to watch carefully to see which birds take the food and what food they take. (An older child could record what happens.)

Some birds may make their nest in your yard. In late fall or winter, when the nests have been abandoned, there is no harm in examining them to find out what they are made of – the materials will probably include twigs, moss, leaves, mud, grass and feathers.

Table top about 150 cm. (5 ft.) above the ground

Corner gaps easier to clean

Wooden

Coconut shell hung on hook

Pole firmly into ground

For birds, too, you could show pictures (or use Montessori biology cards, see page 112) of the different parts of a bird and illustrations of different species, and help your child to identify them. An older child could write about all he has discovered about their life history and feeding habits.

Caring for the family pet This is another enjoyable and educational activity that is suitable for a child between the ages of two and six. The family cat or dog are good pets because they do not have to be kept in cages or hutches. Montessori was very much in favor of freedom and probably would not have approved of rabbits, hamsters and guinea pigs being kept in captivity.

Creating a miniature garden (Age 4 up)
Even if you don't have a yard it is still possible to give your child the experience of growing things – seeds such as beans, radishes, carrots and peas will grow easily in plastic food trays or pots, and whole miniature gardens can be created indoors. Buy a large metal or plastic tray (these are easily obtainable from most garden centers or nurseries) and divide it into sections – four could give you, for example, one of grass, one of miniature bulbs, one of miniature rock plants, and, perhaps, one of radishes. Encourage him to tend to the plants regularly and keep them watered and near sunlight. Windowboxes can be planted and cared for in the same way.

THINGS TO DO IN THE BACKYARD
There is a whole variety of things going on all the time in your yard to provide your child with learning experiences. The following suggestions are activities that could be based around any garden or backyard, and yours will undoubtedly present other, individual, possibilities as well. Look around to spot opportunities, and you, yourself, will begin to see your surroundings in a different, more vivid way.

Observe the seasons (Age about 2 up)
Make a collection of pictures of plants and animals that you know appear in your area during the year. (These can be cut out from magazines and seed packs). Then help your child make a basic plan of your yard. In the spring when the first snowdrops appear, he can stick a picture in the appropriate place on the plan: eventually pictures of crocuses, daffodils and other spring flowers can be added as they appear. Encourage him to look for animals as they come out of hibernation and birds that visit during the season, to watch the trees come into bud and the hedge grow thicker with new, green leaves. Get him to record all these events on his picture of spring.

Keep this picture of spring and discuss it together: the older child can perhaps write a story. Do the same thing in summer, fall and winter, and when you have a record of a complete year, discuss and compare the seasons.

Measuring rainfall (Age about 5 up)
You will need a piece of graph paper for recording, and several empty, plastic bottles. Mark off the sides of the bottles in inches using waterproof masking tape or a waterproof ink marker. Cut off the tops of the bottles, turn them upside down and place them in the base of the bottles (see illustration, right). Have your child place these improvized measuring cylinders in different parts of the yard. At the same time each day, measure how much rain has fallen, and show your child how to record it on the graph paper. Do this over set periods of time to build up a picture of monthly and seasonal rainfall in your yard.

Measuring temperature (Age about 5 up)
You will need a piece of graph paper for recording and a thermometer which can be bought from a garden center. Get your child to place the thermometer in a shaded part of the yard about three feet from the ground. Encourage him to record the temperature at the same time each

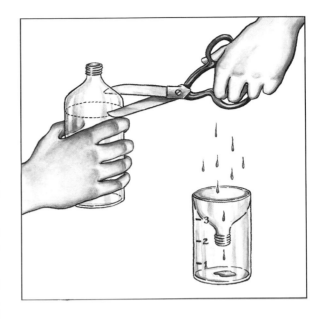

morning, noon and evening. Use the record to discuss temperatures in the context of other weather conditions and generally develop an awareness of the changes that occur during the different seasons. With some children you may continue this for a long time, say over a period of a year.

Recording weather conditions (Age about 5 up)
Make a monthly chart and paste pictures daily of weather conditions, such as sunshine, clouds, rain and wind. Collect weather lore sayings from different countries and teach them to your child, for example, "Red sky at night, sailor's delight, red sky in the morning, sailor's warning," or "Rain before seven, fine by eleven," and test them together to see if there is any truth in them. Encourage him to compare the weather forecast from television and newspaper reports with the actual weather conditions.

PRACTICAL LIFE IN THE BACKYARD
Just as your house requires endless tasks to keep it comfortable and attractive, so does your yard. There is the grass to keep trim, new flowers,

fruits and vegetables to plant, and weeding and watering to be done from time to time. Involve your child in all of these activities as early as possible. Working with him may take you more time, but it will be infinitely more enjoyable and will provide another opportunity to build a good relationship.

Helping to cut the grass (Age about 3 up)

Although a child under six most definitely should not be allowed to use a motorized lawn mower, he could be involved in mowing the lawn in other ways – by pushing the wheelbarrow full of grass clippings to the compost heap, for instance. This is an activity even a three year old can do

Helping in the yard provides a wealth of learning opportunities, from how and when things grow, to the practical everyday activities necessary to keep it cultivated.

provided he has an appropriate-sized wheelbarrow and you supervise him properly.

Planting the bulbs, annuals, and shrubs (Age about 4 up)

Involve your young child in planting by showing him very slowly and carefully how to prepare the ground, then how to put in the plants and water them. Make sure he has appropriate-sized tools. Discuss the seasons with him and what is planted when and why.

IN THE PARK

Originally a park was an enclosed area used for hunting by the nobility; nowadays it is more often a large area of natural environment within the confines of a city or town open to the public. Parks can often be the only "countryside" an urban child will have easy access to, so in order to foster a real love of nature in your child, it is important to take him often to a park and let him play there and enjoy it.

For those who do not have a yard, many of the activities suggested in the previous chapter could be carried out in a local park. But even those who are lucky enough to have their own yard should take their child to the park in any case because the environment will be different, very probably, with a wider variety of trees, plants and animals. There is usually a children's play area, which provides an opportunity for sharing and playing with other children.

GOING TO THE PARK

Getting to the park can be a learning experience in itself. It may involve walking through the local streets, for instance, and it is a good opportunity to introduce road safety.

Start by discussing traffic and, together, talk of all the different vehicles on the road. On a rainy day you might look through old magazines and newspapers and cut out pictures of cars, trucks, buses and bicycles, etc., to see how many different kinds of vehicles you can collect. Stress all the time that traffic is dangerous because it is moving fast, and that sensible people are careful to stay on the sidewalk unless they want to cross

the road. Do not aim to frighten him but try to teach him to be cautious. Remember that as adults we have learned to assess the speed and distance of moving traffic, but this is a judgment that has developed with experience slowly over the years.

To give your child practice, involve him in games that will help him to notice the movement of vehicles and to begin to make judgments. Standing at the bus stop, when the bus appears in the distance ask him to guess how far he can count up to before it arrives at the stop. Make him aware of the importance of sound in judging distance. Again, at the bus stop, ask him to close his eyes and tell you when the bus arrives by the loudness of the noise.

Learning about road safety should begin very early. Your child is absorbing all the time and learning, among other things, to be very careful.

Of course, the most effective way of helping your child make judgments about when to cross the road is to give him lots of practice when safely with you, holding your hand. Always cross roads at the permitted place, either pedestrian crossings, traffic lights or marked crossings. Give him practice in telling you when it is safe to cross.

Never allow your child to play ball in the street, and be careful about letting him hold a powerful dog on a leash in traffic.

The age at which you allow your child to go out on his own will vary and, of course, it is your decision. However, experts recommend that you should never allow a child under seven out on his own on the street as he will simply not have developed as yet enough skill to make the right judgments. You can introduce a child much younger than seven to a crossing code.

THE CROSSING CODE

1. First find a safe place to cross, then stop.

2. Stand on the sidewalk, near the curb.

3. Look all around for traffic and listen.

4. If traffic is coming, let it pass. Look all around again.

5. When there is no traffic near, walk straight across the road.

6. Keep looking and listening for traffic while you cross.

A game to play indoors to underline all of this, is the Road Safety Game (see page 118).

AT THE PARK
A whole variety of activities can be built around visits to the park, and while they will vary according to the individual amenities provided, and the approach of your particular one, the following should be possible in most cases.

Animals in the park
To start with, make a game of observing, naming and counting how many different animals there are in the park. This can be followed by a discussion about which ones are wild, how and why they live in the park, where they live, what kind of food they eat, and where they get it from. Later, at home, an educational activity consistent with Montessori practice would be to collect pictures of the different animals and teach your child how to classify them according to the different groups in the animal kingdom – for example, mammals, birds, fish, reptiles and insects (see page 111).

Or you could concentrate on one animal and together make a storybook all about it. A typical one could be a squirrel. It is a mammal because it has skin covered with hair, and it gives birth to live young squirrels. It has a backbone and is a rodent with short limbs, a long bushy tail and its head is pointed. It can be red or gray. It is a tireless eater, collecting nuts and storing them, and lives in a tree.

Over a period of time, make a study of all the animals you see on your visits. Use your local library to find out facts about them, and encourage him to help find the appropriate books. On a rainy day you can show him how to make a collage of all the different animals you have seen in your local park.

Plants in the park
Trees There will be a much wider variety of trees in your local park than there is in your yard. On one of your first visits, get your child to make a collection of all the different types of leaves he can find. When you get home, you can identify them and teach him the names of the trees they have come from. Depending on the time of the year you can also collect the fruits of the trees, such as acorns and berries. Older children will be interested in knowing other facts about trees, such as that they are the largest plants in the world and they live the longest. Also, that they can take as

much as 250 gallons of water per day from the soil, that they cover about one third of the earth's surface, and that they are very necessary for life because they absorb carbon dioxide and give out oxygen, which practically all living things need to survive.

For more information on trees introduce and play with the relevant Montessori botany cards (see page 111).

Flowers On another occasion you could identify and name all the different flowers you find, and divide them into cultivated and wild ones. At home you could teach your child about the different parts of a flower and explain the process of pollination.

Feeding the ducks in the park can help children gradually to realize the interdependence of all living things.

Recreation in the park

Parks provide amenities for people living in towns and cities. Usually many different kinds of recreational activities are available there, and these often include a children's playground, horse riding, boating, swimming, football, tennis and, occasionally, an ice rink. There is often an area where live entertainment can take place, such as a stage or a bandstand. Encourage your child to watch and participate in at least some of these activities. In addition to helping him acquire physical skills, they will teach him social ones as he mixes with other children and families.

IN THE COUNTRYSIDE

For those lucky enough to have reasonable access to it, the countryside provides the best means of all to experience the reality and joy of the natural environment. Even if it is not possible to take your child into the country regularly, you should try to arrange it so that he does at least see it occasionally, perhaps as part of a vacation.

From an early age, you can bring about an awareness of the importance of conservation and the necessity to respect our environment and the property of others. A good way of doing this is to observe the following guidelines:

THE COUNTRY CODE

- Guard against all risk of fire.

- Close gates.

- Keep dogs under control.

- Use defined paths across farm land.

- Do not damage fences, hedges and walls.

- Do not leave trash.

- Safeguard water supplies by not polluting streams and rivers.

- Protect wildlife, plants and trees.

- Use caution on country roads.

- Respect the life of the countryside

A WALK IN WOODLAND OR FOREST

If you live near, or can drive to, a woodland or forest and can spend a few hours going for a walk, it will provide a whole wealth of new opportunities for you to extend your child's knowledge of nature.

A larger variety of plants and animals live in woodlands than in any other part of the country-side, and you can repeat the activity of listing the names of trees, flowers and animals you find growing and living there.

In a deciduous woodland, for instance, you can observe and identify trees such as oak, ash, birch, beech, sycamore and maple. At waist level there might be bracken and bramble and, at ground level, mosses, lichens, liverworts and flowering plants. Animals in this type of woodland will include badgers, foxes, rabbits, voles, ants, flies, beetles and spiders, and among the birds there is likely to be doves, robins, pheasants, wood-peckers, sparrows, and wrens.

In a coniferous woodland you are likely to find a single type of tree such as spruce, Scotch pine, juniper, larch or Douglas-fir and the ground will have a dense carpet of needles. There are not likely to be many shrubs, and the birds that are found are those that feed on cones and insects such as woodpeckers.

You can talk about the importance of trees and how we depend on them because they absorb carbon dioxide and give out oxygen. Or you could make a leaf library, or a leaf collage, or tell your child how we find out the age of trees by counting the number of rings on the trunk.

At home, you could try to grow your own tree. Find an acorn and soak it overnight in warm water. The next day, peel off the hard outer shell. Plant it in a garden pot, put stones at the bottom, pile some soil on top and then add water until the soil is moist. Place a plastic bag over the pot and fasten it shut to keep the moisture in. The pot should be kept in a sunny place and checked from

The countryside is full of surprises and the fascination of watching living creatures in their natural habitat appeals to young children. Sharing these experiences with your child is important.

time to time. When the seedling appears, take off the plastic bag, make sure you keep the soil moist and put it on a windowsill or in the yard. In the late summer or early fall plant it into the ground.

Another fascinating woodland activity is a "listening walk." This can be done at any time of the year, and for parts of the walk you can close your eyes and stand still. There will be a variety of sounds: bird songs, the rustle of leaves in the wind, small animals scurrying in the undergrowth and the snapping of twigs. If you have a tape recorder you can record these sounds and have your child try to remember what they were when you get home.

On another occasion you could take your child on an "animal kingdom walk." This will involve finding a suitable place to sit for a while so that you can wait and listen for movement. Often the edge of a wood is a good place as this is where you can find rabbits and plenty of insects. Look out for signs of animals, droppings, footprints, pieces of fur and animal homes, such as nests and squirrel dreys. When you get home, your child can make a collage by using cutout pictures and drawings of all the animals he saw in the woods.

Investigate water life in streams and ponds. You will need an ordinary kitchen strainer and a plastic container such as an empty ice-cream carton. Look under stones around the pond or stream and try to find small insects. To use the strainer put it in the water, take it out again and see what you have picked up. Put your findings into the ice-cream carton while you observe and investigate and then put everything back. Make a note of what you find, but remember to always put them back.

A "plant kingdom walk" will yield similar possibilities to collect specimens, such as leaves, flowers, moss, lichen and bark from trees. After you have identified them with your child, take them home and show him how to make bark rubbings (see page 120), press flowers and draw pictures of the things collected.

An activity to do when walking on paths and nature trails is to look for human and animal footprints. These can be recorded in plaster of Paris (take some with you on the walk). In the Turn Over Game (see page 112), there is a section about footprints which would be a useful reference for identifying the prints.

A WALK ALONG THE SHORE

Coastlines can be very varied. Some may be sandy and warm, others may be made up of pebbles and rocks, and yet others may have cliffs. Most shorelines have a wide variety of birds, animals, and plant life. (Among the animal life you can find limpets, periwinkles, mussels, sea anemones, shrimps, crabs, and sea urchins. The most common plants will include seaweed, water pennywort and wild thrift. On sandy shores you can find worms, and sand eels. Many of the coastlines are rich in sea birds, such as gulls, oystercatchers and cormorants.)

You could also make a collection of shells and pebbles, press the plant life and make a shoreline collage. The shells and pebbles can be sorted into groups: shiny or dull, rough or smooth, rounded or sharp, as well as by color, weight and size. By doing this together, you will be giving your child a good preparation for future lessons in mathematics.

Finally, the sea itself has infinite possibilities. You can watch the boats bobbing up and down on the water and talk about where they came from and where they might be going. You can observe the Floating and Sinking Game (see page 68) in action by identifying objects that have sunk to the seabed and those that still float on top of the water. The waves and tides of the shoreline provide yet different learning opportunities and are dealt with more fully later in this book (see pages 128 and 129).

PONDS, STREAMS, RIVERS AND LAKES

Make a freshwater aquarium and collect from the local pond some plant life, water snails and tadpoles. After your child has watched them grow and change, take them back to their natural habitat. This is a good time for learning about lifecycles. The Turn Over Game depicts the life history of a frog and a butterfly (see page 112).

Investigating ponds, streams, rivers and lakes will widen your child's experience of natural habitats. You might like to take him fishing, and while sitting on the riverbank, there will be opportunities to observe animals and birds such as herons, bitterns, loons, grebes, mallards and ducks.

Wasteland

Visiting inner city wasteland and dumps, and observing the types of plant life along a railroad track also provides a variety of learning situa-

tions. Always be sure children are supervised when they go to such places. Many plants and animals have adapted to living in industrial areas – pigeons, sparrows and starlings can be found in cities, and common plants include ragweed, lupin, clover, morning glory and plantain.

Another activity that can be carried out in these surroundings is to observe pollution. Once you have discovered the extent and type, you can then discuss together effective ways of eliminating and preventing it.

Sometimes vacant lots can be used to good effect. City farms such as this one can often give urban children their only real glimpse of country life.

IN THE CITY NEIGHBORHOOD

VISITING THE SUPERMARKET

Many families shop weekly at a local super-market. When you next visit yours, take your child with you and involve him in helping to locate the various items you want to buy; by the time he is five or six, he can help select the most economical items. On returning home, helping to sort, stack and put away will also provide your child with opportunities to learn. You could ask him to check off the items you have purchased on your receipt as you unpack, and if he is interested, he might try adding up how much you spent on meat, dairy products, fruit and vegetables.

The question of where food comes from and how it gets to the shop is another obvious area to explore. Rather than having your five year old respond to the question: "Where does milk come from?" by answering "a supermarket" because that is the only place he has seen it and gets it from, help him make a timeline or wheel (see page 116) to trace the stages between the cow and his breakfast table. He will begin to understand the effort and the organization involved. He could then try to create similar wheels for other favorite foods, such as fruit or even cakes.

VISITING A LOCAL MARKET

Some places still have local street markets, either daily or weekly, general or specific. With their brightly colored stands and noisy crowds, they can be particularly informative and fun to wander around. Counting how many different kinds of one sort of food is available can lead to discussions about which countries they all come from and how food from faraway countries gets here still fresh.

(Left) Selecting her favourite fruit is enjoyable and educational for this little girl. Before long she will be reading the words "apples" and "grapes", as well as telling her mother how much they cost. It's more fun than sitting in the trolley and not being allowed to "touch" anything. (Right) Visiting local places, such as this transportation museum, can provide many opportunities for learning and sharing experiences in the city.

At home you could cut out pictures of different fruit and vegetables, mount them on cardboard, and match them to the different countries on the Montessori world map or play Frutty or Legumo (see pages 107 and 108).

NEIGHBORHOOD VISITS

One of the advantages of living in an urban or suburban community is the number of different amenities and places of interest that are close by. Your local newspaper, radio station or city hall can usually supply details. Such places can include children's museums, art galleries and local institutions like the firehouse or the police station, or perhaps you could arrange to visit a local factory or plant to watch complex industrial machinery in action.

Visiting the local firehouse can usually be arranged, for instance. They might prefer a group of children, so you could get together with one or two other families. The children will be shown the fire engine and all the various appliances it has for putting out fires. The station staff will usually squirt water from the hose, which is great fun for the children. They will explain what happens when an emergency call comes in and if one occurs while you are there, then the older children can check how long it takes for the firemen to get on the fire engine and leave their station. The firemen will talk to the children about the sorts of calls they get. It is always surprising to learn that fighting fire is not the only job they do – they very often have to help people get out of locked apartments.

On returning home you could talk about all the safety precautions you take in your house to prevent fire and tell your child what to do if you unfortunately have one.

Dentists, clinics and hospitals may be located in the neighborhood, too, and since your child will probably need to attend one of them at some point, it is a good idea to foster a positive attitude to what happens there. There is plenty of published literature to help you explain simply the functions of each one and what will happen to him if and when he has to go.

GOING TO SCHOOL

INTRODUCTION

Sending your child to school for the first time can be a daunting experience for you, let alone for your child, and will occur when he is about two and a half or three years if you are sending him to kindergarten. There are, of course, different types of kindergarten and where you choose will depend on your circumstances and preferences. You may choose a play group, a nursery school attached to an elementary school, an independent kindergarten school, a Montessori nursery, or some other type of provision.

The physical aspects of going to and from school – walking along streets, crossing roads, following routes – are dealt with in previous chapters of this book. So, too, are the important issues of encouraging independence in your child and fostering his desire to learn through allowing him enough freedom. Here, therefore, I will concentrate on the equally important help you can give him as he learns to adapt to his new environment.

Wherever you decide to send him, remember that as a parent you must continue to have confidence in your ability to contribute to your child's education and, from the outset, you must try to establish a good rapport with the teachers. They will certainly want to cooperate with you and will have been trained to do so. Learn to have trust in them and to "let him go." Remember, too, that the education of your child from now on will be a partnership between you and his teachers.

Different children respond in different ways to the experience of school, depending on a number of things, which will include personality and temperament as well as the previous experiences he may already have had in being away from home. Some children may become very anxious, and in this case it is important to agree with the teachers how to handle the situation so that, between you, you can build up his confidence. Up until this point you will have done your utmost to build your child's self-esteem by allowing him to "help himself" whenever possible; now that he is going to kindergarten, you can help him to maintain that confidence in himself if you encourage him to do the things that are expected of him.

Bear in mind the following guidelines as you prepare him for kindergarten:

- He should be toilet trained, and he should be able to dress and undress himself when he goes to the toilet. Do not send him to kindergarten in clothes with complicated fastenings.

- Give him as much experience as you can of playing with other children before he goes so that he is not overwhelmed when he first joins the group.

- Build up his confidence in talking to other adults before he goes and, if possible, give him the opportunity of making friends outside the family.

- Prepare him for his first day. Take him to the kindergarten ahead of time so that he is familiar with the surroundings, and introduce him to the teachers and other children.

- Never talk about him to the teacher in his presence in a derogatory way. If you have any concerns, make an appointment with the teacher, put your point of view and ask her/ his opinion.

Parent-Teachers' Association

A good school will have regular parents' meetings, and there may be a Parent-Teachers' Association that you can join and become involved in. Apart from the obvious educational benefits for your child, it will also provide an opportunity for you to meet other parents in your neighborhood.

HELPING YOUR CHILD TO LEARN TO READ

Should you teach your preschooler to read? This is a question asked by many parents. You will find that professional opinions vary. There has been so much research offering conflicting evidence that teachers themselves are still debating which is the most effective approach to use – "look and say" or "phonics," to mention just two. Other areas of conflict are whether or not a child needs to have reached a certain mental age – I.Q., if it helps if he knows the letter names first, at what age should phonics be taught, what about perceptual skills. Reams have been written about the subject of reading, and it is not my intention here to explain all the processes involved, or the different approaches used in helping a child to learn to read.

What is important for parents to know is that preschoolers can and do learn to read successfully and, where parents participate in the process, the results are even more likely to be good.

The Montessori approach has long been successful in teaching children to read at around four. Originally Montessori, working in Italian, devised a phonic method where children learned in simple steps. The English language, however, is not as regular as Italian – to start with there are 26 letters in the alphabet and as many as 44 sounds. If you teach the phonic sounds of "C" "A" "T" he can easily string them together and read "CAT," but what happens with "COUGH"? To read this word, he has to learn other rules. So a modern Montessori approach has now been devised based on recent research,

Reading aloud with your child is a particularly valuable activity. She will learn to love books and stories as well as enjoy your company.

and if your child goes to a Montessori school, he may be using it. I have described the early activities of this reading program on page 60, and you can begin to start the reading process when your child is ready.

There are several specific ways in which you can help your child get ready to read.

Enriching language

Before attempting to encourage your child to learn to read, be sure that you are giving him lots of enriching language experiences. Talk to him as much as possible, involve him in conversation, teach him new words, and tell and read stories to him. Show him that reading is an enjoyable experience so that he learns to love books. While sitting on your lap looking at the pictures of a story, he will eventually begin to notice the words, and may recognize some of them. Involve him in the story by encouraging him to ask questions and tell you what is coming next. Children like the same story repeated over and over again.

Action songs, finger-play stories and rhymes

By being actively involved, children understand the meaning of words, and sentence construc- tions are enhanced. Songs, too, often introduce children to new words and help them to hear the sounds in words more easily.

Words in the environment

Another way of attracting him to the written word is by pointing out written words in the environment. On the bus or train, for instance, there will be signs to read, and in the supermarket different sections will be marked in writing.

Drawing pictures

Encourage him to draw pictures and tell you about them. Then you can write underneath "This is Mummy in her new dress" or whatever is appropriate. He may even read it back to you.

The value of reading

Use your local library, and while taking out a book for yourself, take him to the children's section and let him choose his own book. Visit a book store and let him browse through the children's section there. Developing a good attitude to reading is very important, but, remember, never put pressure on him to read. It will come naturally.

Games and activities

Many of the games in this book will develop visual and auditory perception skills which will help prepare your child for reading. The other games mentioned in the Reading Section will introduce phonics and early reading and writing skills using the Montessori approach.

Mathematics is all about relationships in the world around us; what better way for this boy to discover mathematics than to measure the table in relationship to himself?

HELPING YOUR CHILD TO LEARN MATHEMATICS

Mathematics is all about relationships in the environment and the abstract symbols we use to express them so that we can communicate with others. For example, three oranges is more than two.

A young child reaches the stage of abstraction gradually, but first he must have *experience* of the physical world, followed by learning the *language* to describe the experience. Finally he learns the *symbol* – the word or the number – which represents it.

There are many reasons why children often experience difficulties in learning mathematics in school. In this book I have concentrated on what can be done in the home to prepare him to learn more easily.

He must have as much freedom as possible in the world around him so that he can build up knowledge about it. He needs to be able to touch things, to move them around, to compare them, to climb under, over, on top of, until he begins to get a good idea of the size of things in comparison to himself.

Learning about *numbers* involves three stages

The first skill that needs to be developed is sorting into *sets*. Before your child can identify, say, three cars as being part of the same "set," he needs to understand why they belong together, and in order to do this, he needs to be able to recognize the properties cars have in common.

Another activity is *matching* or *pairing* one set of objects with another set. The child needs to be able, for example, to see that there is one shell in this set and one stone in this set, and here is another shell and another stone, matching them together in pairs. Once he can do this, you can tell him we call this "one" shell, "two" shells, etc.

Another necessary skill is that of *comparison*. This means that a child needs to understand that four stones are greater than three stones, and three stones are greater than two. Once he can see this, he can put things in *order*.

The reason for explaining these educational concepts here is so that you can understand the steps involved and the experiences needed in a play situation prior to the formal learning of "number." Many parents teach their children to count by rote learning, and it is quite common for a three year old to be able to chant the numbers from one to ten. However, many of them will not be able to identify two, or three or four objects.

Activities played at home in an informal way will provide the experiences necessary to prepare your child for formal number work, which will be introduced in a Montessori kindergarten school between the ages of three and four, using Montessori number rods. The timing will depend on when your child is ready, so the more experiences he gets at home the sooner he is likely to be ready.

Another important area of mathematics is the measurement of length, weight, volume and capacity, and there are many opportunities to provide examples of these at home. When cooking, for example, you can encourage your child to count, measure and weigh the ingredients.

Shape and space are other mathematical experiences that can be developed at home, starting with simple activities like matching saucepan lids to the correct saucepan. Many of the games and activities suggested throughout this book provide an enjoyable way of learning about these concepts.

HELPING YOUR CHILD TO LEARN SCIENCE

Science at its most basic is about finding out and understanding about everything. It is also about how things work and change in our environment. What better place to start learning about these than in and around the home? For specific suggestions of opportunities in the kitchen and bathroom see the earlier chapters in of this book; and for examples in the yard and surrounding neighborhood, see the relevant chapters earlier in this section.

From about three years onward your young child will start asking "why" all the time and by the time he is six, you will not know some of the answers yourself.

The stages of scientific development have already been described at the beginning of this section, but the spectrum of experiences will include learning about the variety of life, the processes involved in life itself, human influences on earth, types and uses of materials – to mention just a few.

HELPING YOUR CHILD TO LEARN HISTORY

History is about everything that happened in the past and, again, the home and the neighborhood is a good place to start. The right attitude to learning any subject is important, but in the case of history it is essential.

Children have wonderful powers of imagination, and many people believe that these powers should be channeled into "make believe" worlds, such as playing moms and dads or into the realms of fantasy, such as "teddy bears having picnics in the woods." In contrast, Montessori suggested that these powers should be used to imagine the real world, and she recommended that subjects such as history and geography – which deal with ideas that are beyond the immediate world of young children – be taught in this way.

Essentially, understanding history involves understanding time and putting things into sequence. To do this, children can investigate change, observe differences in living conditions and styles over the ages, and begin to understand the difference between fact and fiction. It is a good idea always to introduce a topic, starting with something relevant and familiar to your child in his own life, and then help him to gather information from libraries, museums, bookshops, historical sites and television programs in order to build up a picture of how people lived in the past.

HELPING YOUR CHILD TO LEARN GEOGRAPHY

As mentioned above, Montessori felt that your child could call upon his great powers of imagination to think about people and places far away.

Start by giving your child a good understanding and knowledge of the area he himself lives in, then broaden this to other areas, helping him to identify the similarities and the differences between them.

Physical and human geography are among the various aspects of this subject that can be investigated. He can also start to develop geographical knowledge in the home, backyard and neighborhood – skills such as following directions, observing his surroundings, inquiring about how the world is made and making simple maps, can be part of everyday life.

HELPING YOUR CHILD DEVELOP CREATIVITY

Encouraging creativity is an important side of your child's development because art activities provide a means of self-identification and self-expression, as well as providing opportunities for intellectual, physical, social and emotional growth.

When he first begins to create, it is important to allow him free expression and plenty of opportunity to explore different materials and mediums. Here the process is more important than the end result.

None of the suggestions above are particularly time-consuming, and most can be incorporated into your child's everyday life. Remember the time you yourself spend with him will help to make his learning experiences more rewarding and enjoyable.

Encourage your child to draw or paint whatever she sees or feels. As well as developing creativity, it helps to develop concentration.

GAMES AND ACTIVITIES

LANGUAGE AND READING GAMES

"I SPY" IN THE YARD OR PARK, OR LOOKING AT NATURE

AGE 2 TO 3 YEARS

How it helps your child
This game is familiar to everyone, but it is particularly good for preparing children to listen for sounds in words. If you get your child used to the phonic sounds before he is taught them in isolation, it will be easier.

What you need
Just to be in the yard or park to play the "I spy" game.
A box of objects, such as a cat, a dog, a pen, a cup, etc., for the other game.

How to play
1. In the traditional game of "I spy" you say to your child "I spy with my little eye something beginning 'r'," and he has to guess what it is that you can see. The thing you are referring to in your mind's eye has to be present so that the child with whom you are playing can use his powers of observation to see it and to name it. If you are in the backyard, for instance, you may be looking at a "robin" which is the "something beginning with 'r'."

2. The game can be varied so that you are giving your child experience in listening for initial sounds, e.g. "I can see a bird beginning with 'b' (blackbird); middle sounds, e.g. "I can see an animal with the sound 'a' in it" (cat); end sounds, e.g. "I can see a flower ending with the sound 'p'" (tulip).
   Don't forget to take turns so that the game is reversed and your child has you guessing, too!

3. Other phonic games can be played in almost any situation – at the airport, in the park, while riding on a bus or going on a car journey, for instance. If you want, you can use objects to help your child learn specific sounds. For example:
   i Put out two objects such as a cup and a pen and say to your child: "I am looking at the one that begins with a 'c'."
   ii Next lay out a few objects such as a cat, hat, mat and a lid and ask him to say the names of the objects and tell you which is the "odd one out" – it is the lid.

MONTESSORI FARM GAME

AGE 3 TO 4 YEARS

How it helps your child
This is a valuable game for developing language skills.

What you need
Model farm buildings and animals
A felt mat on which to lay out the animals
Phonic and nonphonic reading cards

How to play
The game can be played in three stages.
Stage One is purely a language enrichment activity.
1. The child lays out the animals and moves them around the farm, talking about what is happening.

2. You can move, say, the cows and take them from the barn to the field and ask what is happening.

Stage Two is played when your child is first reading easy three-letter phonic words, probably around the age of four, such as man, cat, dog, pig, hen, can, run, sit.

1. You lay out the objects – man, cat, dog, etc.

2. Give your child the corresponding reading cards and ask him to sound out the words.

3. He then places the cards by the objects.

4. Eventually he can make a sentence, e.g. "the man is wet."

Stage Three is for an older child from say five on, when he is reading well and the words he can read are not necessarily phonic but are longer, with more complex sound patterns. He plays with the farm and makes up sentences, e.g. "the man is taking the pigs to the sty."

DIXI
AGE 4 TO 6 YEARS

The game can be played in its simplest form at first, and then it can be made more complex as the child get older.

How it helps your child
This is a game that enriches your child's language development. It is particularly helpful as it develops vocabulary, listening and communication skills, encouraging the child to use whole sentences, all of which are important preparation

Two children play Dixi; in doing so, they communicate with each other and learn new words.

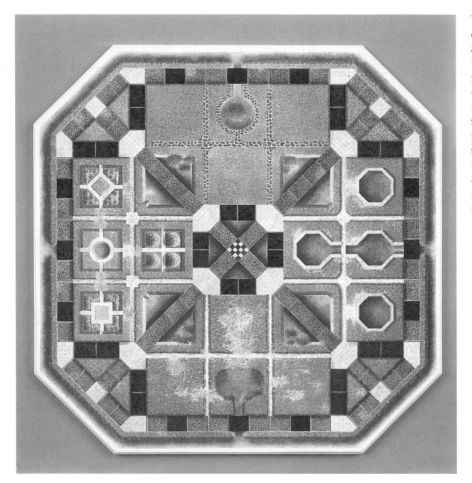

The gameboard for Dixi can be simplified if you are making it at home. Draw in the sixteen squares as indicated, dividing each set of four with a diagonal path of smaller squares (for the pins to move along). The small dark squares in the middle and at right angles to the outside of the board on the left, should be purple.

for reading. It is also designed to be played in a group, which develops cooperation.

What you need
This game is available commercially or can be made at home.
Octagonal game board divided into 16 squares. There are also diagonal "paths" on the board, some squares of which are purple (see photograph above).
4 pins and a dice
48 picture squares depicting the following: house, ball, giant, hut, bag, car, bridge, box, boat, television, telephone, tree, mouse, window, hat, frog, boy, camera, bird, man, broom, cheese, witch, street, doll, elf, banana, purse, airplane, clock, sun, fish, book, rose, lion, mirror, ocean, cat, bed, cage, dog, girl, letter, cake, woman, suitcase, moon, elephant.
To make the game at home, cut out pictures of these objects from old magazines and make a board from cardboard. If you don't have the small pins, you could use colored counters from another game.

How to play
For 2 to 4 players
The first step is to help your child become familiar with the different pictures, making sure he can identify and name them. He might also be encouraged to talk about the possible relationship between two pictures, such as a cat and a

window. For example, "the cat was looking through the window," or "the cat jumped out of the window."

Introductory game

1. Select 16 pictures and place them face up on the squares on the game board. The remaining pictures should be laid face up beside the board.

2. Each player chooses a pin and places it in the center of the board.

3. Throw the dice to see who starts the game. The highest number goes first. The first player throws the dice and moves down one of the diagonal paths, say three places. If the player has landed on a purple square, he takes the picture adjacent to it.

4. He also selects a picture from beside the game board and tries to make up a logical sentence, e.g. "the woman ate the banana."

5. If he is able to make a sentence, he keeps the pictures.

6. Then the next player has a turn, and so on until all the pictures have been taken.

7. If one of you lands on another player's pin, the pin is sent back to the middle of the board. The winner is the player with the most pictures.

Variation for younger children

To make the game more specific to your home situation, confine the pictures to objects which are familiar to the children. Use pictures of household appliances, furniture, foods, plants, people they come across, and pictures of the children themselves, parents and other relations, pets, etc., so the stories and sentences they make up have a relevance to their own experience.

Variation for older children

The game can be made more difficult for older children by requiring them to take more pictures in order to make up a longer sentence or even a short story. If the sentence or story is not feasible another player can challenge by saying: "I doubt it." The player with the pictures is given one more chance to make a sentence or has to return the pictures to the board.

SENSORY DEVELOPMENT GAMES

SORTING FRUIT AND VEGETABLES BY TASTE, TOUCH, SMELL AND SOUND

AGE 2 TO 3 YEARS

How it helps your child

At this age a child responds to everything with his senses. He is learning new things, gradually building up knowledge and vocabulary. All the different ways you can think of to help him learn about fruit and vegetables you usually eat in the family will add to this knowledge.

What you need

A collection of fruit, say, apple, orange, lemon, banana, strawberry, etc.
A collection of vegetables, say, carrot, broccoli, lettuce, potato, leek, spinach, etc.

How to play

1. Line up one each of the above fruits or vegetables.

2. Let your child pick up each one, feel it, smell it, perhaps shake it to see if it makes a noise and describe it.

3. Then suggest he closes his eyes and, one by one, you put the fruit or the vegetable in his

hand and ask him to tell you all about it. You can ask questions like: "Is it smooth?," "What does it smell like?," "Do you like it?," "What is it?."

4. With fruit you can cut a piece out of each one and ask him to taste it and then tell you what it is. Children love this game.

HERB SMELL JARS
AGE 3 TO 4 YEARS

How it helps your child
This activity draws attention to different smells of herbs either grown outdoors, in pots on the kitchen windowsill or bought in the super-market. It increases your child's vocabulary and gives him new knowledge.

What you need
Save old spice jars until you have eight. Then either pick herbs you have grown, or use ones you have bought.
Make up four pairs of smell jars with, say, oregano, tarragon, rosemary and mint. Do not label the jars.
Smell jars can also be bought commercially.

How to play
1. With his eyes closed, ask your child to smell the jars and pair them.

2. Then he can name them.

3. Later he could perhaps match the smells to either the real growing plants or a picture of them.

Touching, tasting, smelling and listening are all ways of finding out about fruit and vegetables. To turn it into a game, ask your child to close her eyes and guess which type she has in her hand. Help develop her communication skills by asking her to describe it.

4. Discuss what the herbs are used for, and let him experience the difference in taste when they are added to certain food.

FRUTTY
AGE 4 TO 5 YEARS

How it helps your child
This game helps your child become familiar with a variety of different fruit and also helps language development and visual perception. It is a good game to play after handling the real fruit and identifying them through the senses.

What you need
4 game boards
48 small cards: 24 with pictures of whole fruits and 24 of sliced fruit
The fruit are apricot, carambola, kiwi, mango, peach, pomegranate, apple, cherry, lemon, orange, pear, red berry, avocado, grape, lichee, papaya, pineapple, strawberry, banana, grape-fruit, mandarin, passionfruit, plum and watermelon.

When the fruit cards have been matched to their board, you can then try to identify which sliced fruit goes with which whole fruit.

How to play
For 2 to 4 players
1. Give each child one or two game boards.

2. Place the fruit cards upside down in the middle of the table.

3. In turn, each child picks up a fruit card and tries to match it to a picture on his large game board.

4. The games ends when one of the children has filled up his game board.

5. A variation to the game can be played using sliced fruit as well as whole fruit.

LEGUMO
AGE 4 TO 5 YEARS

How it helps your child
As with Frutty, this game helps your child become familiar with more vegetables and develops language and visual perception.

What you need
4 game boards
48 small cards with pictures of vegetables, 24 with whole vegetables and 24 with sliced vegetables
The vegetables are artichoke, eggplant, beet, celery, broccoli, carrot, cauliflower, pepper, cucumber, fennel, garlic, lettuce, leek, onion, paprika, potato, pumpkin, radish, rhubarb, cabbage, beans, corn, tomato, zucchini.

How to play
For 2 to 4 players
Play as for Frutty (above), including the variation in step 5.

LISTENING WALK TAPE
AGE 5 TO 6 YEARS

How it helps your child
Apart from the obvious reason of making a walk in the country or park more interesting, you can help your child to become more aware of the world around him and teach him new things.

What you need
If you have a tape recorder, you can make a recording and take it home for a follow-up discussion; but if you don't have one, you can go on a "listening walk" just the same.

How to play
1. On your walk you can either decide not to talk at all and just listen to everything you hear and try and recall it later, or you can stop regularly, sit down and wait and listen.

2. Then ask your child what sounds he has heard and ask him to tell you what he thinks the noises might be. In the woods, or on the beach, this kind of walk can be very rewarding and fun.

3. Later he can listen to the tape and tell you what he remembers about the walk.

MATHEMATICAL GAMES

SORTING AND MATCHING SHELLS AND STONES INTO SETS
AGE 2 TO 3 YEARS

How it helps your child
Develops pre-number skills.

What you need
A collection of shells found at the beach when you go for a walk on the shore or stones found, perhaps, in the yard or the park.

How to play
1. As your child is handling the shells and stones, talk to him about the similarities and differences. What makes a stone a stone? Can you find another stone like this one? Or, what does a shell feel like and what shape is it?

2. Then give him two empty containers, such as empty shoe boxes or small baskets, and ask him to put all the stones in one box and all the shells in another.

3. After doing it with his eyes open, he can try doing it with his eyes closed or with a blindfold on.

4. Later you could suggest he sorts the stones or shells according to size, shape or color.

5. Many variations to these activities can be devised by a parent because there are countless opportunities throughout the day for sorting different things.

SORTING ACTIVITIES WITH TWIGS AND FLOWERS
AGE 3 TO 4 YEARS

How it helps your child
These activities give your child more practice in ordering.

What you need
A collection of natural materials found outdoors in the yard or on a walk in the neighborhood.

How to play
With, say, the twigs collected, ask your child to find the shortest one, then one that is a little longer and so on, till he has put them all in order by length. You can also do this with flowers, selecting the shade of the petals or the size of the stem.

COLOR AND COUNTING LOTTO
AGE 4 TO 6 YEARS

How it helps your child
This activity develops a variety of skills, including color matching and number recognition. The child practices recognizing numbers by counting the quantities and then associating the proper number with them. The material can also be used to give him practice doing simple sums.

Description
10 pairs of color-coded scenes of chickens (as here) or other animals on cardboard.
Sets of cards, each with a numeral, mathematical sign such as plus or minus, or dots printed on them (see photograph overleaf). The dot cards should correspond to a numeral card (1 to 10).

How to play
1. Begin by matching the pairs of animal cards, using color as a guide.

2. Count the number of chickens or animals on each pair of cards.

3. The number card for that quantity can be associated with the pictures.

4. Now match the number card with a card with a corresponding number of dots.

5. Arrange the paired number and dot cards in their sequence from 1 to 10.

6. Add the mathematical sign cards to the game now by putting the correct one with relevant number and dot cards to make up the totals.

7. Use other combinations, independent of color, to create different sums. Use more than two colored cards to create yet other sums. The order of pictures and symbols can also be changed to make still more combinations.

SCIENCE AND NATURE GAMES

PICTURES OF THE NATURAL ENVIRONMENT
AGE 2 TO 3 YEARS UP

How it helps your child

After a walk in the countryside or even time spent in the backyard observing nature, you can look together at pictures or books about the natural environment. Encourage him to talk about the pictures he sees and give him new words and information.

You can supplement his learning by making label cards to be placed next to the pictures, and you can use the Montessori botany and zoology cards (see opposite), to teach your child more about each plant and animal.

How to play

You can make this into a game by sticking the pictures on cardboard and then cutting each of them up into four, six or eight or more pieces, to make a puzzle. He can then play with the pieces alone by putting the pictures together again.

(Top) In Color and Counting Lotto first match the chickens by color then identify the number of chickens there are. The numbers can then be arranged in order from one to ten.

(Bottom) Later, the numbers can be associated with the same quantity of dots – and, later still, the total can be made up from two smaller quantities of dots.

CLASSIFICATION CARDS OF ANIMALS AND PLANTS

AGE 3 TO 4 YEARS

How it helps your child
These pictures of animals and plants expose your child to a variety of living things, providing opportunity for discussion which will increase his knowledge and help language development.

What you need
Make a collection of pictures. These can be cut out from old magazines or cheaper books.

The animals could include a variety of mammals, birds, fish, reptiles and insects.

The pictures of groups should be mounted on color-coded cards so that when they are sorted into types, your child can check to see if he has sorted them correctly.

The plants could include pictures of cultivated and wild flowers. Again these could be mounted on to color-coded card.

Montessori zoology and botany cards can easily be prepared at home (see below for specific subject ideas).

Trees
Set 1 – Parts of the tree
Set 2 – What leaves do
Set 3 – Tree flowers
Set 4 – Fruits and seeds of trees
Set 5 – Animals that live in trees
Set 6 – Plants that live off trees
Set 7 – Uses of trees

Flowers
Set 1 – Parts of the flower
Set 2 – Insect pollination
Set 3 – Wind pollination
Set 4 – How seeds grow
Set 5 – How flowers and insects work together

The starting point of animal classification is recognition of similarities and differences. Here, the young girl is matching picture cards of different animals. Later, she will be able to sort them into groups according to similarities, such as those that are mammals or birds, and so on.

How to play
1. This is an activity that should be introduced after your child has actually been out with you and looked at either animals or plants in their natural setting, if this is at all possible.

2. Sitting with your child, go through the pictures of the different animals, talking about them and telling him what group they belong to and what it is about them that distinguishes them as a bird, insect, reptile or mammal. Name the animals and talk about where they live and what they eat.

3. Then let your child sort the pictures by himself and check to see if he has done it correctly.

4. Do the same thing with the pictures of plants.

BOTANY AND ZOOLOGY CARDS – PARTS OF ANIMALS AND PLANTS

AGE 4 TO 5 YEARS

How it helps your child

These activities help your child acquire more knowledge and increases his vocabulary.

What you need

Sets of homemade cards depicting different parts of animals and plants. Choose animals such as a rabbit, a cow, a bird, an insect, a tortoise, and for the plants, I suggest you start with a flower, a leaf, and a tree.

First draw the outline of the animal, bird, or plant, then trace it five or six times.

On the outline of each card, color in one part of, say, the bird, i.e. the breast, the head, the beak, the wings, the legs (see photograph).

Make two sets of each animal or plant, and a set of reading cards naming the different parts of each one.

How to play

1. The first activity is for your child is to match the cards and name the parts.

2. Later he can read the words "breast," "head," "beak," "wing" and "legs" and so on, and place these reading cards beside the appropriate pictures.

TURN OVER GAME

AGE 5 TO 6 YEARS

How it helps your child

These activity cards increase your child's knowledge of things in nature and help him develop new concepts. They also encourage logical thought and problem solving.

What you need

A circular board with removable colored pieces around the outside (see photograph).

Two-sided "exercise" cards showing on one side a selection of, say, animals and their homes, animals and their tails, animals and their tracks, the life cycle of a chicken or a frog, the steps involved in becoming a butterfly, and so on. Center drawings should be color coded to correspond with a removable piece of color (see photograph). The other side should be color coded to the correct pairing or ordering.

How to play

1. Ask your child to select one of the exercise cards and place it on the board. The side with the colored circles in the center should be face up.

2. Ask him to remove the coloured pieces from the rim of the activity board.

3. The child begins with any of the inner drawings, e.g. a parrot (as here), and tries to find its 'home' (the bird cage) on the outer series of drawings.

4. He then chooses the coloured piece that corresponds to the parrot circle and puts it beside the cage. The child continues in this way until all the pieces have been matched and placed round the board.

5. Then he turns over the exercise card and the outside of the card should match the colours on the outside of the activity board. This acts as a control of error.

Turn Over starts as a matching game, putting together animals with their appropriate home (as here). Removable outside colour pieces act as a control of error when the board is 'turned over'.

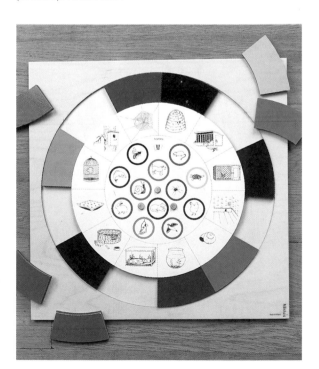

HISTORY GAMES

MEASURING TIME
AGE 2 TO 3 YEARS

How it helps your child
These activities provide experience of measuring short periods of time. At this age few children will be able to count beyond two or three, so we are not expecting to measure the time passed in standard units but rather to let the child experience a period of time in comparison with other things happening in his life.

What you need
Various egg timers, an hour glass. (These activities can be done either inside the house or in the garden.)

How to play
1. Start with a minute egg timer. Let your child watch the sand pass through the glass and then tell him that it has taken one minute.

2. You could suggest that you close your eyes for one minute and he can tell you when the minute is up.

3. Then you could suggest that you do something like fill the watering can from the tap in the garden and see if it takes more than one minute.

4. When he is older you could give him experiences of longer periods of time, such as an hour. Show him how to use an hour glass. Explain that an hour is a very long time.

5. Suggest he does something for an hour and you will see that he keeps checking to see if an hour has gone by because he does not expect it to be so long.

TIMELINE OF THE YEAR
AGE 4 TO 5 YEARS

How it helps your child
It gives a pictorial representation of time and helps a child to build up the idea of a sequence of events.

What you need
A long sheet of either paper or plastic approximately 60 inches long and 5 inches wide (a much larger one can be made if you have the space to display it either in your child's bedroom or somewhere else in the house).
Mark 12 equal sections and label them with the months of the year. (Children of this age in a Montessori school probably will be reading.)
You will also need a collection of pictures (see below), or you can ask your child to draw them.

How to play
You might like to introduce this activity at the beginning of the year or perhaps on your child's birthday, or when something significant happens, such as starting school or moving.

1. Talk about what you are going to do in the coming year, when you are going on vacation, when Christmas and Easter will be or any other events or holidays your family celebrates. Try to find suitable pictures of these events, and place them on the Timeline.

2. At the beginning of each month, talk about what the weather is like, what has happened outdoors, perhaps the leaves are beginning to yellow and fall, etc. You may record other things mentioned in this book, such as the amount of rainfall each month or the temperature outside.

3. By the end of the year, you and your child will have built up a picture of all the things that have happened and you can sit down together and talk about them. Children love to do this, and you will find it interesting to discover the things they remember most.

SHADOWS AND THE SUNDIAL
AGE 5 TO 6 YEARS

How it helps your child
Through observing how shadows move, your child will begin to develop an understanding of how the sun affects the earth, and how we measure time.

What you need
A pole about 8 inches long
A large sheet of paper
A block of wood, with a clock face which you can draw yourself
Most of all, you need a sunny day!

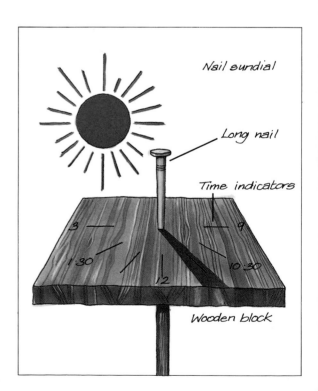

Nail sundial

Long nail

Time indicators

Wooden block

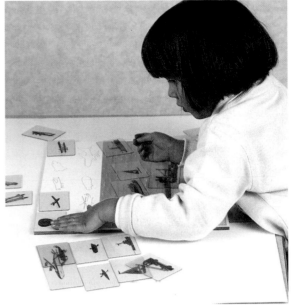

(Left) Different types of transportation are put in appropriate places on land, sea or air.

(Right) The reverse sides of the boards reveal any errors.

How to play

1. Children love to play with shadows. Your child will try to catch his own shadow or yours, and he will try to stand in front of, behind and beside his own.

2. Show him how shadows move by placing a large piece of paper somewhere in the garden, ask him to stand on it and draw around it. Mark the time on the piece of paper.

3. At regular intervals, go back to the same spot and help him draw around his shadow again.

4. Or you could place a pole in the ground and record the movement of the shadow at regular intervals.

5. Make a sundial using the block of wood and a nail. Mark the shadow of the nail at regular intervals, gradually building up a clock face.

GEOGRAPHY GAMES

TRANS
AGE 2 TO 3 YEARS

How it helps your child

This activity extends your child's vocabulary and helps to reinforce travel experiences he may have had after an outing or a journey. It can also be used to reinforce left/right orientation.

What you need

3 activity boards depicting air, water and land on one side and outlines of appropriate methods of air, land and sea travel on the other (see photographs)

27 cards with pictures of varying methods of transportation. If you wish to make up the game at home, you can use pictures cut from magazines.

How to play

1. The first step is to ask your child to match the picture cards to the outlines on the activity boards.

2. Following this you can discuss each means of transport and where you are likely to find it. 'Is it used on land, water or in the air?'. Some of the less obvious ones will be new to young children.

3. The next step is to turn over the activity board to the blank side which only depicts air, land and water. Now ask your child to place the pictures in the right place on the board.

4. He can check to see if he did it correctly by turning the board over again.

5. For older children the other possibilities are to have discussions about how fast or slow the transport goes, or whether it is modern or old fashioned.

6. With children from about 4 years onwards you can ask them to place all the methods of transport facing either the left or the right.

LAND FORMS
AGE 3 TO 4 YEARS

How it helps your child
As this activity is introduced at the *practical life* stage it can be initiated as early as 3 or 4 years. It indirectly prepares your child for much later abstract work in geography, but at this stage it will serve to increase his vocabulary.

What you need
Baking trays
Plasticine or plaster
A jug of water
Make plasticine models of a lake and an island. As your child gets older you may make other land forms such as peninsula, gulf, bay, cape, straights, isthmus.

How to play
It is best to do this activity after an outing when you have seen a lake or visited an island.

1. Show the child how to pour some water into the tray which represents the lake.

2. Then let him do it and tell him an island is a piece of land surrounded by water. With the lake he sees that it is a piece of water surrounded by land.

3. Follow up activities are to look for puddles in the garden that are like lakes, or to make lakes and islands when he is playing in the sandpit or by the seaside.

FROM FARM TO TABLE SEQUENCES
AGE 4 TO 5 YEARS

How it helps your child
Following a visit to the supermarket or perhaps a local farm, or even after a walk when you have looked at the countryside and seen cattle and sheep grazing, or seen wheat growing, you can follow this up with the story of how things get from the farm to the table. You are giving your child information and extending his vocabulary.

What you need
Make up activity cards to go with the 'Turn Over' board. These could be the story of milk and the sequence would be cattle grazing, cows being rounded up for milking, the milking machine, tankers collecting the milk, the bottling plant, the milk van, the milk carton on the supermarket shelf or milk bottles on the doorstep, and finally milk in a jug on the family dining table (see diagram).
Other possibilities are bread and cereal.

How to play
1. Tell your child the story of the journey of the milk and show him the sequence in pictures on the activity card.

Selling Eating Grazing

From farm to table

Bringing in

Bottling

Collecting Milking

2. Then let him play the Turn Over Game (see page 112) and check to see if he did it correctly.

3. Once you have introduced the idea of all the things that happen before food reaches the supermarket shelf and your dining table you will find that your child will begin to ask the question: "Where does this come from?". Also you could make a collection of all the different packages of cheeses and discuss all the by-products of milk.

MODEL TOWN AND MAPPING
AGE 5 TO 6 YEARS

How it helps your child
These activities help your child develop an awareness of spatial relationships and perceptual skills, as well as prepare him for using maps either of your own neighbourhood or of different countries. The activities are also excellent for language development and learning and teaching a second language.

What you need
2 model towns or farms fitted together by a divider (see photograph).
2 charts for each scene
A box of appropriate models. These could include, say, 10 cows, 5 trucks, 5 cars, 3 children, 3 sheep, 5 horses, 3 ducks, 3 chickens, 3 men standing, 3 trees, 2 stands, a bench, a man sitting, a gate post, a bridge, a rooster and a dog.
Activity cards so that a child can play alone or with a friend.

How to play
1. First help your child to become familiar with the models and talk about the scenes.

2. Then set up two identical scenes, either of the town or of the farm.

3. You begin by placing the models on the scene and describing where you are putting each object.

4. Your child tries to copy your actions from your verbal instructions.

5. After a while you can check to see if the two scenes are the same and the models are in the same place.

6. This activity can be reversed with your child giving the instructions.

7. If he wants to play by himself, he can use an activity card and follow a given pattern.

8. After playing this game for a while you could extend the activities by introducing two-dimensional pictures of the objects so that what has been created looks more like a map.

Mother and daughter communicate to each other the scene they have created on their side of the picture divider.

9. Ultimately, your child will be able to draw a map of his own house, yard or neighborhood.

The commercial version of this game, called Dubbledam, comes with a variety of other activities that extend the child's knowledge.

ROAD SAFETY
AGE 5 TO 6 YEARS

How it helps your child
The game will help you reinforce the idea of caution on the roads, and where and when it is safe to cross the road.

What you need
A large sheet of paper drawn with a snake which

is divided into sections. At regular intervals draw different pictures of safe places to cross the road, such as pedestrian crossings, traffic lights, bridges and underpasses. If a player lands on a crossing he can jump a few places up the snake. Also at irregular intervals, draw manhole covers on the snake. These lead the player down the snake back toward the beginning. Another hazard is an occasional banana skin on which a player can slip and have to go back a place (see diagram below).

A dice

2 or more miniature men to show where the players are on the ladder

How to play

1. Each player chooses a man and throws the dice in turn.

① Go back to home
② Wait (miss) one turn
③ Fine to cross – move forward 3 places
④ Go back 2 places

2. The idea is to move up the snake and get to the head first. On the way if you can cross the road at a safe crossing you can skip a few places.

3. If you are unlucky you fall down a manhole and have to move back or start all over again. You may also slip back a place by landing on a banana skin.

ARTS AND CRAFT ACTIVITIES

VEGETABLE AND FRUIT PRINTING
AGE 2 TO 3 YEARS

How it helps your child
In addition to all the reasons given earlier in the book for encouraging art and craft in the home, this particular activity will give your child the opportunity for self-expression and to communicate his ideas. Ideally you could do this activity with leftover vegetables, or fruit, that aren't fresh enough to eat. (You should always be concerned to discourage waste). The activity will also help your child develop new skills.

What you need
Different surfaces on which to print such as coloured paper, newsprint, rice paper, paper towels, plain paper, old wallpaper, or fabrics.
Thick tempera or powder paint
Suitable vegetables such as potatoes, carrots, celery and fruits like oranges and apples
You could also make a printing pad by putting absorbent paper or wet cloth in a shallow dish and then adding the paint.
Use a different dish for each colour.

How to play
With a very young child use the flat surface of a cut vegetable or fruit. They will all make different patterns.

With a slightly older child you can cut out a pattern on the end of the vegetable.
Show your child how to print by dipping the vegetable into the paint and making a row of patterns across the surface of the material you are printing.

RUBBINGS
AGE 3 TO 4 YEARS

How it helps your child
These activities will help your child develop an awareness of the art form such as shape, line, form and colour, and will also develop fine motor skills.

What you need
Different surfaces on which to make the rubbings, such as brown wrapping paper, white or coloured paper
Wax crayons
A selection of objects from which to make rubbings. Choose things in the park or the garden such as bark, leaves, bricks, paving stones.

How to play

1. Show your child how to hold the paper firmly with one hand and the crayon, flat on its side, firmly with the other.

2. Slip the leaf or bark under the paper and rub hard. The results will vary and can be cut out and used in a collage of the environment.

MODELLING AND CARVING WITH NATURAL MATERIALS
AGE 4 TO 5 YEARS

How it helps your child
Modelling, particularly with clay, seems to be totally absorbing for a child. It develops fine motor skills and often appears to have a calming effect. It also helps creativity and self-expression.

What you need
Either natural clay (which is best), plasticine or playdough
For carving, suitable materials are soap, wood or rock salt
Prepare the working surface, carefully protecting the table, or provide a work board or a mat. If you are using real clay the finished products can be baked and saved.
Be sure your child learns how to clear up properly after using clay.

How to play

1. To start with, allow your child to feel the material and see how he can change its shape.

2. Then show him how to roll it out, knead it, twist it, push and pull it into shape.

3. Give him a few ideas to start with by making some simple things and then ask him if he can make something himself.

DESIGNS WITH STRING
AGE 5 TO 6 YEARS

How it helps your child
A child of this age will enjoy experimenting with different kinds of string and rope and this medium can be very creative.

What you need
A variety of coloured string and rope
Choose a fairly hard surface for fixing the string on to, such as card. Dark colours produce good results.
A strong glue

How to play

1. At first let your child explore freely.

2. Then you could suggest a subject or theme such as flowers, a bird or patterns with circles and straight lines. When he has chosen an outline get him to draw it first with glue on the surface.

3. Then show him how to place and stick the string on to the glue.

Discovering About the World

INTRODUCTION

In this section I discuss the ways in which you can broaden your child's horizons by looking at other countries of the world and at the entire universe.

Children these days are much more exposed to the world than they were even fifty years ago. On their television screens each day they are likely to see and hear about people from other countries. They will probably meet people from abroad who may be either friends of the family or living nearby in their community. They may even be lucky enough to travel somewhere overseas on holiday and, from time to time, they will see and hear about space travel.

To stimulate an interest in faraway places the Montessori approach is to start with a simplified version of the globe, and in a Montessori school you will find three year olds handling the globe and naming different continents without any difficulty. Then they will move on to learning more about what it is like in the different countries, starting from something the child is familiar with, such as her own family and home, and relating this to other peoples' families and homes. In this way she begins to realize that she is part of 'the human family'.

We use a hands on approach always, introducing new ideas with concrete objects or pictures for the child to see, touch and manipulate. Eventually more and more abstract ideas can be talked about and you will find, years later, she will tell you something she remembers that you thought was beyond her at the time.

By introducing children to the idea of the 'human family', Montessori hoped to lay foundations for a better understanding of the importance of co-operation and harmony among human beings. Montessori had much to say about world peace. She was nominated for the Nobel Peace Prize two years in succession, in 1949 and 1950, because over a period of seventeen years she had written about and lectured at international conferences on the importance of developing an understanding of the human problem and restructuring human society. She firmly believed that the way to do this was through the child, and that the work of education was to establish a lasting peace. She had many theories on this subject, but the one highlighted here draws attention to the importance of helping young children to develop a caring attitude towards their fellow human beings and encouraging them to foster friendships.

Another way of making it interesting for your child to learn about the wider world is to teach her about festivals around the world. She will not, of course, understand the religious significance behind the celebrations at first, but she will be able to feel a sense of belonging. You can introduce the idea of other children doing other things at their festival – they have special food, special activities and special clothes. In this way you can contribute to your child's understanding of how all the people of the world are different, and gradually develop in her an acceptance of the differences rather than a prejudice against them.

To talk of trips and journeys is an excellent way of firing her imagination and awakening her sense of adventure; I also cover some practical aspects of taking a journey with a child.

The world beyond is our final chapter dealing with the 'family of the sun' – a subject that strongly attracts young children. Many parents may think this is beyond the comprehension of children under six. I can only advise you to introduce some of the ideas mentioned here; soon you will be surprised to find that your child knows more than you do and that she is passionately interested in pursuing the topic.

THE HUMAN FAMILY

THE GLOBES

Start with the globes. There are two Montessori globes. The first is the land and water globe which has the continents covered with sandpaper and the sea painted blue, so that initially the child learns two things – the shape of the world, which is a sphere, and that it is made up of land and water. The second globe has the continents painted in different colours – Europe is red, Asia is yellow, Africa is green, Australasia is brown, North America is orange, South America is pink and Antarctica is white – and the child learns the names of the continents and oceans. (If your child goes to a Montessori school she will most likely be introduced to these globes there, but if she doesn't you can still help her to learn the same ideas from an ordinary globe.)

PUZZLE MAP OF THE WORLD

The Montessori world puzzle map is made up of two hemispheres, each with the continents removable as whole puzzle pieces. The colours are the same as those on the globe. It is easier for a young child to see how the world is represented on a flat map if she can take out the pieces and compare them with the same continents on the globe – the shape, colour and size will match. (This piece of apparatus can be easily made at home by tracing round the continents in an atlas, then cutting them out in coloured paper and sticking them on to cardboard.)

Once your child has learned the names of the continents, you can tell her how they are divided into different countries·which are areas of land with a name, flag and national anthem.

Looking at a collection of pictures of mothers and babies from many different countries (see the game on page 137) provides a talking point for children, and helps them to imagine what it is like to live in another country. The pictures are then matched to the puzzle pieces from the Montessori world map.

When discussing other countries with your child, start with something that is familiar to her such as her own family, and tell her that there are many other families like her, all over the world. In fact, we all belong to the human family. Talk about the things she does every day and what she needs – in the morning she gets dressed, so she needs clothes, then she has breakfast, so she needs food. She lives in a house which shelters her from the cold or from the hot sun, and she has a family who love her and with whom she talks and plays each day. Tell her that in other countries there are young children just like her, but some of them wear different clothes, eat different food and talk a different language.

If you are lucky enough to visit another country with your child, it is a wonderful opportunity to help her learn about it. Try to find out as much as possible about the everyday things that happen there, and encourage your child to ask questions and make comparisons with her own country. Collect pictures, photographs, slides, dolls, folk art, recordings of traditional music, recipes and anything else that is typical of the country you are visiting. When you get back, set up a special area for your collection of things – a shelf in your child's bedroom, for instance. Make a scrapbook of the pictures in a color-coded book (to match the color of the continent) and display the various artifacts. You will probably find that in so doing, you have stimulated her interest in finding out more about other countries, as well.

I suggest you choose one country from each continent and gradually build up a collection of information. For examples, you could choose England from Europe, Kenya from Africa, Malaysia from Asia, Peru from South America, Mexico from North America and New Zealand from Australasia.

EXAMPLE: MALAYSIA
The sort of information you could collect from a country such as Malaysia would be:

Non-Asian children learn to use chopsticks with ease. Visiting ethnic restaurants or preparing ethnic food at home, is a way of helping your child realize that there are many differences in food and eating habits around the world.

Typical pictures showing tropical vegetation and crops: rice, rubber and coconuts, and industries such as tin mining and forestry.

Pictures of the people from the three main cultures – Malay, Chinese and Indian – showing the facial features, different traditional dresses. If possible, try to acquire a Malaysian doll.

Pictures of different houses, from the beautiful modern architecture of Kuala Lumpur to the houses on stilts in kampongs and the long boat-houses jutting into rivers.

Examples of handicrafts, such as batik, papier-mâché and handwoven baskets and hats.

Pictures of animals and plants, such as the fascinating orang-utan, beautiful orchids and exotic fruits such as guava, rambutan and durian.

Recordings of Malay music and perhaps one or two songs that can be learned in the Malay language, which is called Bhasa.

Stories and legends from Asia, such as the famous Malaysian story of how the mousedeer tricked the tiger can be found in libraries and book stores. Embassies might also be helpful in providing sources of information.

These days we can buy food from all over the world, and on one occasion the whole family could eat like Malaysian people do, using typical utensils. Involve your child in preparing and cooking the food and talk about how it differs from our own.

Try to relate all this information to your child's own life so that she can imagine what it is like for a small girl of her own age living in Malaysia.

The pictures could be mounted on yellow cardboard (the color of Asia) and eventually used in the Continent Game (see page 138) or put into a scrapbook which your child could make herself. You will find that she will treasure it and come back to it years later, remembering all the things you told her.

FESTIVALS AROUND THE WORLD
A festival is the celebration of a special event, often connected to a religious belief, and usually there is feasting (festival means feast day), as well as dancing, music and often dressing-up involved.

In most schools the festivals that are normally celebrated in a particular culture will be talked about, and in many cases art and craft work done, and stories and perhaps drama enacted by children to help them learn about their own culture. Making Christmas decorations, Easter cards and masks for Halloween is common practice in the West. In Montessori schools, however, the teachers often introduce unusual festivals when the children are learning about another country. The approach is to find out everything possible about that country, including the people, climate, crops, industry, animals, plants, literature, music, dress, food, stamps, currency and festivals. What is more, it is a hands-on approach – the children actually get involved in their learning, making it easier for them to envisage what it is like to live in that other country.

EXAMPLE: MALAYSIAN FESTIVALS
There are many festivals held in Malaysia, but the following represent the three main cultures: Chinese, Malay and Indian.

The Chinese New Year This is one of the main celebrations in Malaysia, falling in January or February on the first day of the first moon and is celebrated by Chinese Malays. There is usually a week's holiday, and every home is brightly decorated with vermilion "lucky" scrolls inscribed with ancient proverbs in gold Chinese characters. The shops are decorated with dragon-studded signs saying "Kung See Fat Choy" – Happy New Year. The streets come alive with music and dancing dragons. Children dress in their best clothes and receive lots of "ang-pows," money wrapped in red packets.

Make "lucky scrolls," Chinese lanterns, and dragon clothes. Cook Chinese food and try using chopsticks.

Hari Raya is the Muslim festival which marks the end of the fasting month in July and is celebrated by the Malays. There are three days of feasting and rejoicing.

Deepavali falls in October and November and is celebrated by the Hindus, who burn tiny oil lamps outside their houses to signify the triumph of good over evil.

JOURNEYS AND EXPLORATIONS

Journeys provide excellent opportunities for learning. You will have told your child that the world is a very large place, and from the information you have given her about different countries she now knows that they are very varied. She may well have asked such questions as: 'How do you get there?' 'How far away is it?' or 'How long will it take?'

You can introduce the idea that journeys link places and begin to talk about all the many ways you can go from one place to another.

With two to three year olds you can show them pictures of the many different types of transport and play Trans (see page 115).

With three to four year olds you can talk about the journey to school, what kind of transport you use and how long it takes. Try to draw a very simple map showing the route you take, and draw pictures of all the landmarks you pass on the way. If the school is fairly near, try different forms of transport to get there – walking, by car, by bus, by train, or maybe by bicycle. Make a graph of the results (see page 133).

With four to six year olds you can play a holiday game. This could involve discussion about modes of travel, for instance, distances involved, time taken, what weather conditions are needed for different types of holidays, and things to do when you get there.

Actually holidays provide a wonderful opportunity to explore different parts of the country, or to visit other countries.

The journey itself is exciting but often can be very tiring for both children and parents. Remember to prepare well and, during all the inevitable waiting periods, make sure you meet the needs of your child – food, comfort and sleep – and always have plenty of games on hand for her to play.

An airport is an excellent place for exploration. Most of them have visitors' galleries where you can go while you are waiting after check-in and before departure. Airports are usually full of an assortment of people and you can play a game guessing where they come from or where they are going to, looking at their clothes and features and listening to their language. On the aeroplane itself, have plenty of activities ready – books, cards, drawings, miniature board games and perhaps some favourite toy, such as a doll to dress or an action man.

Choosing a holiday is a very individual thing, but with children under six the seaside, country or camping holidays are particularly suitable

Travelling in cramped conditions is particularly difficult for children. One solution is to keep their minds active by providing plenty of suitable books and games.

because there is usually plenty of freedom and lots of things for them to do and explore.

At the beach there are many opportunities for learning new things.

Beach holidays are memorable for young children; there is a sense of freedom often lacking in everyday life. There is time to share the delights of warm sun and sea, as well as explore new natural habitats and investigate what lives in the sand or in the sea.

- Playing on a sandy beach can promote discussions about what happens with water and how sand is different from other soils.

- You can talk about pollution at the oceanside.

- You can go for a walk along the shore and look for shells – cowries, mussels, whelks, periwinkles are just some that are likely to be found. You may also find starfish, sea urchins or sand dollars. In certain areas there may be a variety of seaweed.

- Exploring rock pools will uncover even more unusual living things: snail-like shells stuck to rocks, hermit crabs and limpets. Buy a book about the ocean and read together about all your discoveries.

- If you stay in one place for a week or more, you can ask an older child to make a diary of the tides and see how the times of high and low tides vary each day. You can talk about this as she learns about the earth, sun, and moon (see overleaf).

THE UNIVERSE

Children at the age of five are filled with wonder and enthusiasm for this subject. Start by buying a simple book about space, the stars and planets, and in the form of a story tell her about the "family of the sun." Our planet, the earth, is part of the solar system which consists of nine planets, many moons and thousands of asteroids and comets.

To make this simpler to understand, draw a picture of the solar system on a large piece of paper and display it in your child's room. The sun is more than a hundred times bigger than earth and it provides light and heat. Its powerful force of gravity keep the planets – Mercury, Venus, Earth, Mars, Jupiter, Saturn, Uranus, Neptune and Pluto – orbiting around it.

You can make a set of cards showing a picture of each planet and describing their main features. These can then be used for the Rockets to the Planets Game (see page 135).

Your child will also be interested in astronauts, spaceships and rockets. If you can visit a museum with a good exhibition, this is the best idea, but you can also interest her by finding out together what it is like living in space. How do the astronauts get a supply of air, food and water, and how do they cope with weightlessness because there is no gravity in space? They have to strap themselves in before they go to sleep and, because they float around the spaceship and do not have to make any effort against the pull of gravity, their arm and leg muscles become weak.

Other strange things happen – there is no up or down because there is no gravity: drinks have to be squeezed from plastic bags and the astronauts must drink through a straw. Turning a glass upside down doesn't work – the liquid stays where it was! Astronauts have to wear special clothing to protect them from the unfiltered ultraviolet rays from the sun and from tiny meteorites, which are smaller than particles of sand.

A rocket is a vehicle designed to lift itself into space by overcoming gravity. It propels a fast stream of gas through a nozzle toward earth – it simply "pushes" itself away. To explain this to your child, ask her to blow up an oblong balloon, attach it to a stick with paper clips and tape, point the inflated balloon up and let it go. It will propel itself toward the ceiling and away from her and the floor.

You can make a timeline of the conquest of space: 1957 The Russian Sputnik 1 was the first rocket to go into space; the first human in space was the Russian, Yuri Gagarin, in 1961; in 1963 Valentina Tereshkova became the first woman to orbit into space; in 1965 Alexei Leonov was the first man to make a "space walk" and so on.

It's a wonderful world out there, and you can learn about the universe as you are learning about the world around you.

GAMES AND ACTIVITIES

*LANGUAGE AND READING GAMES
AND ACTIVITIES*

SONGS AND NATIONAL ANTHEMS AROUND THE WORLD

AGE 2 TO 3 YEARS

How it helps your child
Learning new songs will help your child's language development and will also give her a sense of community when she is able to join in with other children.

What you need
A selection of song books, preferably from different cultures, containing songs that are sung at different festivals.

How to play
If you play an instrument, it is an asset, but not a necessity – just sing the songs many times and gradually your child will join in.

COUNTRY SNAP

AGE 3 TO 4 YEARS

How it helps your child
This game develops visual perception and helps her remember salient characteristics of different cultures.

What you need
2 sets of cards depicting people clad in typical native dress or national costumes from China, India, Pakistan, Arabian and African countries, U.S.A., Scotland and any other countries with distinctive style. These could be simple, hand-drawn line drawings.

How to play
The traditional snap game (see page 138).

"WHERE DO I LIVE?" LANGUAGE GAME

AGE 4 TO 5 YEARS

How it helps your child
This game encourages language development.

What you need
A set of picture cards of 10 different countries, each one with a picture of a plain map, say of the United States. Also on the card are pictures of typical scenes or objects from the country, such as a picture of the Stars and Stripes, the White House, a split-level house, etc.

How to play
Deal the cards so that you and your child have five each. You start by looking at one of the cards and describing everything that is on it. Your child has to guess which country it represents. If she gets it right, she is given the card; but if she gets it wrong, she doesn't. Then you can have a turn.

NEW WORDS TO USE WITH THE WORLD MAP

AGE 5 TO 6 YEARS

How it helps your child
It provides practice in reading new words.

What you need
A set of cards with the names of the continents written on them
A map of the world with the continents shown but not named

How to play
Read the words with your child to make sure she can recognize them and then ask her to read them herself and place them on the corresponding continents on the world map.

PRACTICAL LIFE AND SENSORY
GAMES AND ACTIVITIES

SORTING LEGUMES
AGE 2 TO 3 YEARS

How it helps your child
This is an activity that will help prepare her for mathematics.

What you need
A collection of legumes, say 4 different types
4 small dishes and one larger dish
A blindfold

How to play
Place all the legumes in the large dish, put the blindfold on your child and ask her to sort the legumes into the four dishes by feeling them.

COOKING ETHNIC FOOD
AGE 3 TO 4 YEARS

How it helps your child
This practical life activity makes the study of a culture more interesting, as well as giving her new ideas.

What you need
A Chinese wok, some fresh vegetables that she likes (carrots, broccoli, beans, scallions, fresh ginger and so on).

How to play
Using a chopping board, show your child how to slice the vegetables, fresh ginger and scallions into small segments. Heat a tablespoon of oil in the wok and ask her to put the vegetables in just when the oil begins to smoke. After about 3 minutes, add about 2 tablespoons of oyster or soy sauce and serve.

MATHEMATICS GAMES

GRAPH OF JOURNEY TO SCHOOL
AGE 4 TO 6 YEARS

How it helps your child
This activity gives your child experience of measurement skills and provides an opportunity for recording information in pictorial form.

What you need
Graph paper
Pencils or crayons
A watch. If your child cannot tell the time by herself, you will have to tell her how long each journey takes.

How to play
1. Each day of the week choose a different way to go to school: on Monday walk, on Tuesday go by car, on Wednesday go by bicycle, on Thursday go by train or subway, on Friday go by bus. If any of these ways are not appropriate for where you live, or you do not have the necessary means of transportation, estimate how long it will take.

2. When you get home, record the time taken in graph form. This can lead to a discussion about the different types of transportation and the advantages and disadvantages of each one.

SCIENCE AND NATURE GAMES AND
ACTIVITIES

MAKING A PINWHEEL
AGE 2 TO 3 YEARS

How it helps your child
Your child will begin to understand the force of wind, and it is fun.

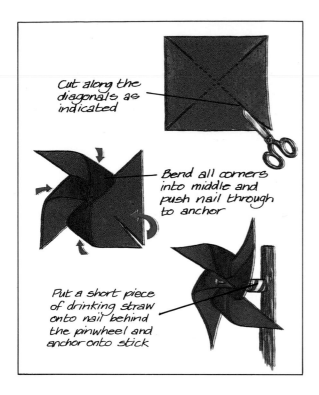

Cut along the diagonals as indicated

Bend all corners into middle and push nail through to anchor

Put a short piece of drinking straw onto nail behind the pinwheel and anchor onto stick

What you need
Some paper – colored if possible, about 6 inches square
Scissors
A drinking straw and a thin nail
A thin dowelling stick about 12 inches long (obtainable from a craft store)

How to play
1. First make the pinwheel by folding the square of paper, corner to corner.

2. Cut along the lines about halfway to the middle, then fold the corners over to the middle and secure with a nail.

3. Cut a small piece of the drinking straw about half an inch long, and slip it onto the end of the nail at the back of the pinwheel, attach it to the stick with the nail.

4. Now ask your child to go outdoors and stand

still, holding the pinwheel high above her head. See if it moves around.

5. Suggest she runs with it to see if it goes faster.

ANIMALS AROUND THE WORLD
AGE 3 TO 4 YEARS

How it helps your child
Develops knowledge and understanding of other countries.

What you need
The animal classification cards (see page 111). Select those that are typical of each continent, for example:
Africa: lion, giraffe, leopard, elephant, zebra, rhinoceros, gorilla, lemur
Australia: kangaroo, koala bear, dingo, wombat, wallaby
Europe: Fox, badger, deer, chamois, weasel, European bison, lynx, gerbil, squirrel, wolf, moose, wild boar
Asia: panda, mousedeer, orang-utan, monkey, mongoose
North America: musk ox, caribou, lemming, buffalo, brown bear
South America: jaguar, giant otter, tapir
Antarctica: polar bear, penguin, seal
The world map

How to play
1. Talk about the different animals and where they come from, what habitats they live in, what they eat and so on.

2. Your child can then look at the pictures and place them on the map in the appropriate continent. (Color-code the cards on which you mount the pictures so that she can check with the colors of the continent to see if she has got it right.)

THE SOLAR SYSTEM
AGE 4 TO 5 YEARS

How it helps your child
Gives her knowledge and understanding of the universe.

What you need
A set of 9 cards, each with a picture of a different planet of the solar system
Another set of cards, repeating the above pictures, but with the names underneath the planets
A set of cards with names only
A set of cards describing the planets

How to play
1. The younger child should just match the pictures, and you can tell her about the different planets.

2. Later when she can read, ask her to match the names on the reading cards with the planets and place them below the correct one.

3. Still later, when her reading is more fluent, she can match from the description cards.

ROCKETS TO THE PLANETS
AGE 5 TO 6 YEARS

How it helps your child
Gives her knowledge and understanding of space travel and is fun to play.

What you need
A picture of the solar system mounted on a game board with 40 squares around the outside perimeter, the corner squares are inscribed Earth, Comets, Moon, Meteors. The nine squares between the corners represent planets and are colored sequentially (see illustration).
Homemade rockets (made to look different from a scroll of paper)

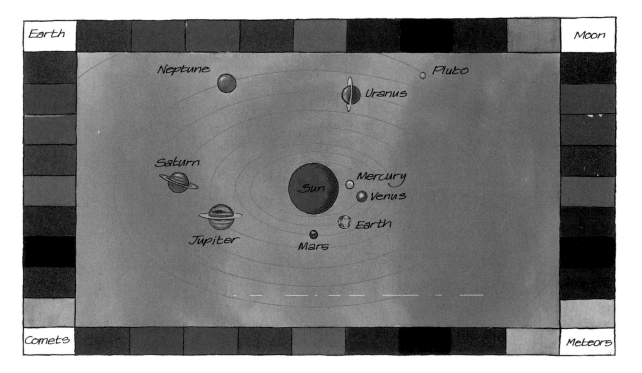

9 sets of color-coded cards with four questions about each planet
4 colored counters or disks for each planet, one placed on each of the planet squares
A dice

How to play
For 2 to 4 players
1. Each player has a rocket.

2. The first player to throw a six starts by placing her rocket on the Earth square and throws the dice again. She moves her rocket along the outside of the board, depending on the number thrown.

3. She will land on a color, so she picks up the appropriate colored card and reads the question. If she can answer the question, she takes one of the colored counters from the planet.

4. Each player has a turn and play continues in this way.

5. If a player lands on one of the two opposite corners Comets or Meteors, she gets an extra dose of energy which gives her the power to take away a counter from another player. If she lands on the Moon, she is very clever – not many people land on the moon – so she has another turn.

6. The object of the game is to get all four counters and win a planet. The player with the most planets wins the game.

HISTORY GAMES AND ACTIVITIES

THE BIRTHDAY GAME

AGE 2 UP (for the two year old, it is just a game, but for older children the activity will begin to make sense).

This child is celebrating her fourth birthday by walking around the candle four times. In so doing, she learns how the earth circles the sun once every year.

How it helps your child
This game provides a first impression of the relationship between the earth and sun, and helps her to realize what is meant by one, two and three years old. This will start her off on building the concept of time. It is a good idea to play it at children's birthday parties.

What you need
A globe
A candle
An oval shape marked out on the floor – with chalk if the floor is suitable, or ribbon if the game is played on a carpeted floor.

How to play
1. At your child's birthday party with a group of friends, ask them all to sit around in a circle, on the outside of the oval you have drawn on the floor.

2. Place the candle in the middle and explain that it represents the sun.

3. Ask the birthday child to take the globe and walk around the sun on the oval line and then back to her place in the circle. Explain that it takes a whole year for the earth to move around the sun.

4. Each time, after she has walked around the path, ask her to stop and tell her a little story about when she was one, two, three, four and so on. If she is four you can sing "Happy Birthday" when she completes the fourth round, etc.

5. To give an impression of years, it is always fun to ask the children at the party to guess how old you are. Then you tell them your real age, and you walk around the sun the right number of times – they can't believe it!

TIMELINE OF FESTIVALS
AGE 4 TO 5 YEARS

How it helps your child
This activity helps to build up the concept of time and sequence by displaying it graphically.

What you need
Use the timeline previous prepared for the Timeline of the Year (see page 114).
Postcards you have collected of the different festivals about which you have talked to your child.

How to play
After each festival you celebrate, for example Christmas or Easter, or after you have been talking about another festival from another culture, glue the appropriate postcard on the timeline.

STORIES OF EXPLORERS
AGE 5 TO 6 YEARS

How it helps your child
Because children love stories, one way of teaching them facts about the past is by reading to them. The stories of some of the great explorers fire the imagination of children of this age and help them to understand events of the past.

What you need
Children's books which are well-illustrated. Appropriate stories are about the Vikings; Marco Polo in the 13th century traveling the Silk Road to China; Christopher Columbus in the 15th century sailing across the Atlantic to America; Captain James Cook in the 18th century circumnavigating the world and landing in Australia and New Zealand; the courage of Captain Robert Scott of the Antarctic; and Yuri Gagarin pioneering travel in space.

How to play
Read a story to your child and encourage her to ask questions and look for places on the map. Encourage her to draw pictures of ships, past and present, used for exploration.

GEOGRAPHY GAMES AND ACTIVITIES

MOTHERS AND BABIES AROUND THE WORLD
AGE 2 TO 3 YEARS

How it helps your child
This activity helps the young child begin to develop an idea of how different people look and behave.

What you need
Sets of pictures collected from magazines, travel

brochures, museums, and information centers. Pictures of mothers and babies that are typical of different cultures and countries from around the world

Mount the pictures on color-coded card and keep them in the appropriately colored folders – the colors should match the colors of the Montessori continents map.

A map of the world

How to play

1. Show your child one folder at a time, looking at the pictures together and talking about the different features, clothes, what they are doing, and ask questions; i.e., whether she thinks they live in a hot or a cold climate.

2. On another occasion show her a folder from another continent and so on until she is familiar with all the pictures you have collected.

3. Eventually, she can take out the pictures by herself, find the right continent, take out the puzzle piece and place the picture by it.

TRANSPORT SNAP GAME
AGE 3 TO 4 YEARS

How it helps your child
This game helps increase the child's knowledge and awareness. It is also a good vocabulary activity as she is probably learning new words, and the pictures may lead to further discussion about transportation.

What you need
2 sets of cards depicting different methods of transportation.

How to play
The game is played in the same way as the traditional snap game, with each player holding half the pack, cards face down and putting them out face up one at a time, taking turns. When two cards are the same, the first player to call "snap" takes both cards. The winner is the one who ends up with all the cards.

FLAGS AROUND THE WORLD
AGE 4 TO 5 YEARS

How it helps your child
This activity increases your child's knowledge about different countries.

What you need
A map of the world
2 sets of pictures of national flags to make flag cards (they can be bought from a Boy Scout or Girl Scout center), or flag stamps can be obtained commercially to go with Montessori maps of the world.

How to play

1. Start with a few flags, teach your child where they come from and let her match them in pairs.

2. Show her how to place the right flags on each country on the map.

THE CONTINENT GAME
AGE 5 TO 6 YEARS

How it helps your child
This game is played by older children, because they should now be familiar with continents and countries, and the different aspects of culture they have learned about in earlier activities suggested in this book. The game reinforces this knowledge.

What you need

A large, rectangular game board, with a map of the world in the middle.

48 squares around the edge of the board are randomly colored red, blue, yellow, green, orange and purple. In the four corners of the square there are danger zones: the first is a home, the second is a volcano, the third an earthquake and the fourth a tidal wave. Halfway between each corner are "environmentally friendly" zones: the first is a tree planting area, the second a recycling plant, the third a solar energy station and the fourth an endangered species animal reserve (see illustration).

6 packs of cards in the same colors as the squares; i.e., red, blue, yellow, green, orange, purple. On the front of these cards are sets of pictures of countries, animals, homes, plants, clothes, food. The cards are placed color side up in the center of the board.

6 bingo cards, one for each continent, the Americas (North and South), Europe, Africa, Asia, Australasia, Antarctica

6 miniature replicas of means of transportation, i.e., a car, an airplane, a ship, a bicycle, a train, a bus

A dice

How to play

1. Each player chooses a method of transportation and a continent.

2. The first player to throw a six starts the game. She throws the dice and moves around the board the number of places indicated on the dice. She will land on one of the colored squares, say a red one. She then picks up a red card and looks at the picture; if it corresponds to her continent, she takes it and places it on her continent card. If it does not correspond with her continent card, she replaces the card underneath the red pack.

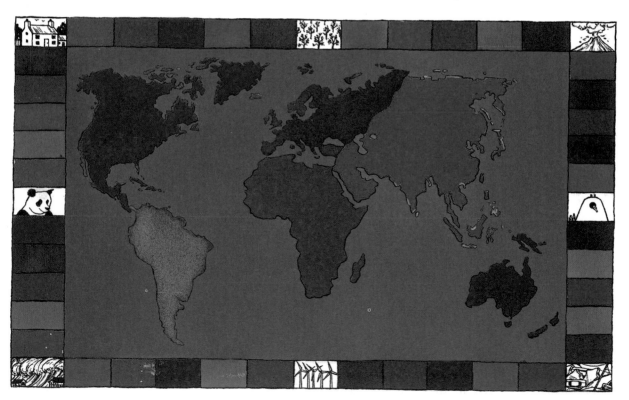

3. The game continues in this way with the players moving around the board as they throw the dice.

4. If they land on a hazard such as a volcano, earthquake or tidal wave, they have to go "home."

5. If they land on a bonus area – i.e., any of the four "environmentally friendly" zones, they get an extra turn.

6. The winner is the player who fills up her continent card with one of each of the colored cards.

ART AND CRAFT ACTIVITIES

PAPER CUTTING
AGE 2 TO 3 YEARS

How it helps your child
This activity encourages manual dexterity and also prepares your child for more difficult craft work.

What you need
Thin cardboard (of similar weight and thickness to birthday cards). Prepare graded cards by drawing lines with a pen where the scissors are meant to cut. The first card should consist of simple straight lines, the second card should have straight lines with rounded corners, and the third card curved lines only.
Scissors

How to play
1. Show your child exactly how to hold the scissors and how to cut.

2. Give her progressively more difficult shapes to cut out, and eventually give her thinner paper, which is not as easy to cut.

MAKING FLAGS
AGE 3 TO 4 YEARS

How it helps your child
This activity increases her knowledge and gives her practice in pencil control.

What you need
Typing paper and a ruler
Crayons
A flag book for reference

How to play
1. Draw different flags for your child to color in. Start with the flag of your country.

2. Later introduce other flags, and when she has finished them, she can paste them in a scrapbook.

PAPER FOLDING – ORIGAMI
AGE 4 TO 5 YEARS

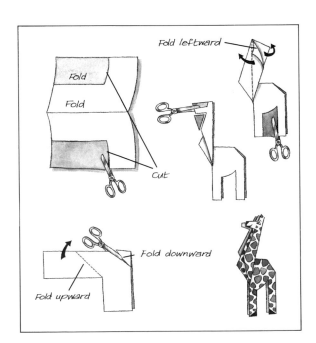

How it helps your child
This activity improves manual dexterity and provides an opportunity for creativity and imagination.

What you need
Colored origami paper from a craft store
Scissors

How to play
1. Begin by practicing folding paper in half and then in quarters.

2. Select a subject that can perhaps go with one of the countries about which you are talking to your child. Animal Origami is fairly simple.

3. To make a giraffe, for example, fold the paper as shown opposite, below.

CANDLESTICKS FOR HANUKAH
AGE 5 TO 6

How it helps your child
This activity encourages creativity and improves manual dexterity.

What you need
8 toilet paper tubes
Strong card
Poster paint
Silver or gold paper

How to play
1. For your candlesticks cut two cardboard shapes (Diagram A). Make two slits upward from the bottom of the candlesticks.

2. Paint your two cardboard candlesticks with poster paint. You can paint on the branches of the candlesticks, or glue on strips of gold or silver paper.

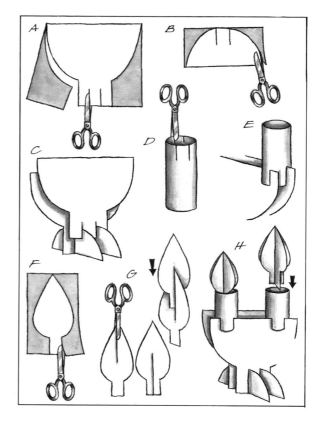

3. Cut two cardboard shapes (Diagram B). Make two slits downward from the top of these. Paint these two shapes with poster paint.

4. Assemble your candlestick (Diagram C).

5. To make your candles, cut four short slits at one end of each toilet paper tube (Diagram D).

6. Paint your candles with poster paint.

7. Put your candles on your candlestick (Diagram E).

8. For each candle you will need two flame shapes (Diagram F).

9. Make slits on the flames (Diagram G) and push them together. Finally, put a flame into each candle.

INDEX